The Afterlife Unveiled

What 'the Dead' Tell Us About Their World

The Afterlife Unveiled

What 'the Dead' Tell Us About Their World

Stafford Betty Ph.D.

BOOKS

Winchester, UK
Washington, USA

First published by O-Books, 2011
O-Books is an imprint of John Hunt Publishing Ltd., Laurel House, Station Approach,
Alresford, Hants, SO24 9JH, UK
office1@o-books.net
www.o-books.com

For distributor details and how to order please visit the 'Ordering' section on our website.

Text copyright: Stafford Betty 2010

ISBN: 978 1 84694 496 3

A CIP catalogue record for this book is available from the British Library.

Design: Tom Davies

Printed in the UK by CPI Antony Rowe
Printed in the USA by Offset Paperback Mfrs, Inc

We operate a distinctive and ethical publishing philosophy in all
areas of our business, from our global network of authors to
production and worldwide distribution.

CONTENTS

Acknowledgments   ix
Introduction   1

Chapter 1 Trance Teachings from the
        Seventh Sphere   11

Chapter 2 The Afterlife of a Young Texan   25

Chapter 3 A Notable American's First Year
        on the Other Side   36

Chapter 4 A Psychical Researcher on This Side
        Speaks to Us from the Other Side   48

Chapter 5 A Catholic Priest Describes the
        'Land of the Great Harvest'   61

Chapter 6 Oh, the People We Meet Over There!   75

Chapter 7 What the Protestant Theologian
        Discovered upon Dying   88

Conclusion   102
Afterword   116
Key References   119
Select Bibliography   120
Index   123

There can be few, if any, more important questions than what happens to us when we die. This book contains what purport to be reports from people who have died, telling us in what conditions they live, and how they may move on from one sphere to another. Whatever they may make of this, everyone will find it intensely interesting.

John Hick, author of the classic *Death and Eternal Life*, preeminent philosopher of global religion

After conducting a pattern and content analysis of details that spirit sources described about their afterlife world through credible mediums, Dr. Betty spells out 44 specific details of the afterlife, most of which differ from the views of major world religions. Belief in these revelations that the nature of our afterlife existence depends upon using our free will to evolve spiritually in love and wisdom in this life is the core message of this book.

Boyce Batey, Executive Director, *Academy of Spirituality and Paranormal Studies*

The foundation of organized religion is life after death. Yet, orthodox religion has failed to paint a picture of an appealing afterlife. There have been, however, various accounts of the afterlife coming to us through sensitives who have penetrated the veil. In this book, Professor Betty gathers together some of the most intriguing and interesting accounts, offering us a more realistic picture of both the higher and lower realms.

Michael Tymn, author of *The Articulate Dead*, Vice-President of the *Academy of Spirituality and Paranormal Studies*

If you are looking for a book about the afterlife viewed through the lens of mediums, this is the one to read. Dr. Stafford Betty has carefully studied many of the significant mediums in history and presented a composite of information they have received from sitters of various backgrounds. You will find some of the most fascinating and controversial accounts of the nature of the afterlife without the usual academic jargon. There is so much to ponder and discuss you will not be able to put this book down.

Louis LaGrand, Ph.D.
Author of *Love Lives On*

Acknowledgments

Thanks to Brett Books for permission to quote from Ruth Mattson Taylor's *Evidence from Beyond*; to Stephen Chism for permission to quote from his book *The Afterlife of Leslie Stringfellow*; and to the editors of *America Magazine* for permission to reprint my article "Life after Death Is Not a Red Herring."

I wish to thank Thomas Berry, my mentor at Fordham University who introduced me to the wide and spacious world of comparative religion; to John Hick, the world's preeminent global theologian whose point of view I found irresistible from the start; to Huston Smith, the world's dean of religious studies whose unearthing of forgotten truths lit a fire in me that could not be quenched until this book got written; and to Michael Tymn, who has investigated the world of the medium as thoroughly and meticulously as anyone alive.

Many scientists, on the other hand, tell us not to pay attention to such 'messages' because there is no such thing as spirits and life after death. Other people take a middle path, including some of the world's best scientists. They bring a critical but open mind to the topic. That is the attitude I take and encourage you to take.

What exactly is a medium, and what do mediums do – or claim to do? They are gifted people, more often than not women, who are able to stop their minds from thinking and feeling – blanking them out, if you will – so that a spirit can make use of them. Some mediums go into a trance, either deep or shallow, while others remain awake and aware of what is coming through them. Some write out the message, while others speak or even type it out. Almost all first-rate mediums marvel at what comes through them. Often ideas or points of view totally alien to them turn up. Often information comes through them that they had no way of knowing. This information, they claim, doesn't come from theological surmise or philosophical argument, but from spirits directly telling us about the world they now call home.

Mediums such as John Edward, the TV celebrity, are famous for ostensibly putting deceased relatives in contact with their grieving relatives. Spirits use his mind to communicate their presence and prove to the grief-stricken that they are still very much alive, and usually quite happy. We are not interested in this kind of communication. Here we will be studying communications that describe the world in which the spirits live – and that presumably we will go to when we die. What you make of them I cannot predict. But I think that many of you will be amazed at what you find. Wherever they come from, they are fascinating and often inspiring. They reveal an astral world of amazing beauty and stepped-up intensity of thought and emotion; an overall plan that explains not only the spirits' purpose over there but ours right here; and a mysterious grandeur that surpasses the ability of our language to describe it adequately. The feeling of being thrilled by the orderliness, justice, and magnitude of the divine plan it lays out; of seeing with clarity what is expected of us here and now, and what the consequences of success and failure are; of coming to know that death is not the end, but that a mighty world lies just ahead; of glimpsing a personal future that inspires, here and now, a dedicated commitment to bettering our own world – all this, and much more, comes through these readings.

Christians are starved for more clarity about the afterlife. I know several who go to church faithfully but don't even believe in an afterlife, so implausible (they feel) is the Church's account of it. Heaven, hell, and maybe purgatory – so medieval, so Dante-esque – can it really be like that? Then there is the other extreme: tit-for-tat reincarnationists who insist that everything that happens to us is karmically necessary and therefore just – from the earthquake in Haiti to the flat tire you get on the way to the airport. I believe that conventional beliefs regarding life after death are antiquated and that this book will bring them up to date. And for those believers, or would-be believers, who are troubled by the secular bias against all talk of a spirit world, there is even better news. What they read here is likely to bolster their hopes, perhaps dramatically. Nihilistic materialism and atheism, one of our young century's most woeful pathologies, is contradicted at every turn by our spirit friends.

There is, of course, no finally conclusive evidence of what to expect when we die. But the messages here, from different times and backgrounds, are consistent with each other. After reading several dozen of these accounts, you can almost predict what the next one will say. This fact suggests that they are revealing a real place or state, for what else could account for the similarities among the accounts? Hikers on a mountain trail will notice many different things along the way, but after listening to all of them tell their story, it won't take long before you realize they are talking about something they all really experienced, not something they each separately dreamed up.

Other factors point to the same conclusion. Helen Greaves, one of the mediums we'll be getting to know (Chapter 6), wrote after reading what came to her in a light trance:

My pen scarcely lifted from the page. When I read through what I had written my astonishment grew. This happened for several days and I became more astounded at the subjects upon which I had written. I could not, without effort and without definitely searching my limited imagination, have invented such stories as poured through me.

She goes on to explain, 'There was hardly a correction made in all the hundreds of words written, though I was never aware of what I was going to write.'

In the first chapter we'll meet one of the greatest mediums in history, the English clergyman Stainton Moses. Though not in trance, he was completely unaware of what he was writing. He explains:

I cultivated the power of occupying my mind with other things during the time that the writing was going on, and was able to read an abstruse book [held in the left hand] and follow out a line of close reasoning while the message was written [by the right hand] with unbroken regularity, [with] no fault in composition and often a sustained vigour and beauty of style.

This points with some force to another mind doing the writing through Moses' hand.

In still other cases, the handwriting of the medium is not her own. And in the case of voice mediums, the voice is not her own. The celebrated Irish medium Geraldine Cummins, the subject of this book's fourth chapter, produced about fifty different person-alities, handwritings, and literary styles in her career, many chance that all or even most of the mediums featured in this book are conscious frauds. But there is a slight, a very slight possibility that all seven accounts have been unintentionally fabricated by their subconscious imaginations. We know what elaborate stories patients sometimes tell their hypnotists when they are regressed!

Though confident that much, even most of this material is authentic, I am less confident that everything you read here came through exactly as the spirit communicators intended. For there is the ever-present danger, as we just saw, that the medium cannot be trusted to be a completely uncontaminated receiving station, and will instead unintentionally let her own ideas intrude and corrupt the message. My own view after reading complaints by communicators is that this does sometimes happen, though usually not to such a degree that the overall meaning is crucially tainted. I am very nearly convinced that *most* of what you read here really came from the Other Side and came through accurately; in other words, that it is a true revelation. Once you see how similar the accounts are, in spite of coming from sources so far apart, I think you will be inclined to agree.

These accounts are potentially useful for two types of people: the dying and the healthy – in other words, just about everyone! *Testimony of Light*, the book I end my Death course with at the university where I teach, and the subject of Chapter 6, creates a real stir in my students. Fundamentalist Christians and Muslims often dislike it, and hard-core materialists usually express contempt for it. But the majority of the class are intrigued, and more than a few have told me it's the most important book they ever read, for it tells them not just what to expect when they die but, more importantly, *what the purpose of life is here and now.*

What of the dying or the very old who read a book like this for the first time? If I had made a bad job of my life, I would be concerned; I might even prefer extinction to the afterlife world described here. But for a decent person with a few months to live, this book would be, I am sure, a godsend. The otherworldly visions of dying patients that are recounted by hospice nurses produce great joy and peace in the dying, and the near-death experience almost always removes the fear of death from the one who has it. It is hard to imagine a greater blessing for people close to death. All the better if we not only lay aside our fear of becoming nothing when we die, but have something concrete that we can look forward to. Mediumistic accounts of the world awaiting us at death provide just that. I'll bet that most of you who believe in an afterlife have only the vaguest notion of what it will be like. That's unfortunate; such vagueness chips away at faith, and faith is what we need at death. There is nothing vague about the afterlife world revealed here. You could even make a movie out of it – as Robin Williams did a few years ago (*What Dreams May Come*, based on Richard Matheson's well-researched novel by that title).

These accounts would also be good for society at large. They make it clear that our station in the afterlife depends on the kind of person we choose to be in this life. If taken seriously by the whole society, the confident expectation of accountability would have a profoundly salutary effect on it. No one could be happy about landing in the Shadowlands, or the Realm of the Unprogressed, or the Lower Astral found in these accounts. And most of us are humble enough to admit that we need a karmic prod every now and then to keep us from degenerating into unethical selfniks.

On the other hand, the vivid, beautiful, attractive worlds awaiting the good would provide a strong positive incentive – the carrot rather than the stick – for virtuous action. All these accounts point out the importance of forgiving each other while still in the flesh. All make it clear that a famous name or big bank account means nothing in the world to come. All emphasize the spiritual growth and eventual happiness that come from handling life's hardships with grace and dignity. These accounts make it clear, vividly clear, that there is a direct cause-effect relationship between virtuous living in this world and a happy life in the next.

Many people today, especially our youth, resort to bad behavior because they don't see any harmful consequences coming from it. If they did, if they *had a map* showing what the consequences were, they would be more careful. If a whole society knew that no one ever got away with bad behavior – from rape or character assassination to fighting or gossiping or just plain laziness – far fewer would allow themselves such license. Virtuous behavior emphasizing humility, kindness, honesty, courage, forgiveness, self-control, dedication to purpose, and self-sacrifice might become habit-forming. And our world would be much, much happier for it.

I look forward to the day that authentic mediumistic literature will become more widely available and more universally respected. The best parts of the world's several scriptures deserve to endure, but the worst provoke exclusivism and generate misery on a vast scale. In addition, no scripture comes close to revealing what truly awaits us when we die. The world is hungering for something better, something that can serve as a reliable revelation that knits together people and cultures rather than dividing them further. Anyone who reads this book is likely to come away feeling that life is meaningful and good, and that each of us has an important part to play in its proper unfolding. Authentic mediums might well be the closest thing to the voice of God that our planet has.

The Protestant reformer John Calvin thought it wise to resist the temptation to say much about the afterlife, since the Bible says so little about it. Others, including several of my friends, both atheist and Christian, are convinced that it's impossible to know what, if anything, follows death. We are like fish swimming in the ocean, unable to know what might lie above it. Having an opinion about the afterlife is as silly as thinking we understand what it's like to live on some extra-galactic planet.

This stance, while becoming in its modesty, is unnecessarily defeatist. As we will see, the afterlife world is nearby, and there is no reason it should remain forever inaccessible to us. It is not light-years away, but as close to us as dark matter. In any case, the advice of these naysayers is being ignored today, and rightly so, by millions of curious seekers, of all ages, whether near death or not, who are discovering the literature of afterlife – from books about the near-death experience (NDE), to accounts by the slowly dying who report seeing visions of the world to come, to the ever-growing literature said to come from the dead themselves speaking through mediums. This last kind of literature is the focus of this book.

In the chapters that follow, the actual words of the spirits will appear in bold print. The seven chapters are presented in chronological order. As pointed out earlier, you will find quite a bit of repetition – what you would expect of a world the spirits share rather than some sort of fabrication from each medium's subconscious. Then again, there is enough dissimilarity to suggest that there are many levels or spheres in the Afterworld. It is clear that the communicating spirits do not all exist at the same level. A 20-year-old Texan (Chapter 2) who begins to communicate shortly after his death is not likely to live in the same realm as the English co-founder of the Society for Psychical Research who died at a more advanced age and has been dead for 20 years (Chapter 4) when he comes through. Their descriptions reflect their different backgrounds and life experiences. For the reader, this divergence could be important. Chapters 1, 4, and 7 will appeal to the more philosophical reader interested in the laws governing the Afterworld, while Chapters 2, 3, 5, and 6 will probably appeal to the reader more concerned with the landscape, geography, and technology of the Afterworld. There is no need to start with Chapter 1 just because I did. Each chapter can stand alone.

In the concluding chapter I will put all this information

Chapter I

Trance Teachings from the Seventh Sphere

You will learn hereafter that the revelation of God is progressive, bounded by no time, confined to no people.
Imperator

The most gifted and remarkable English medium of the nineteenth century was an Anglican minister named William Stainton Moses (1839–92). At first Moses frowned on the strange mediumistic phenomena he had heard about. And like so many of his fellow clergymen, he looked upon communication with the dead as demonic. But after attending his first séance, during which the medium gave a remarkably accurate description of a deceased friend of his, his skepticism waned. Within months he became aware of his own psychic gifts, including the ability to produce – he didn't know how – extraordinary phenomena, especially levitation. On one occasion he was thrown onto a table, and from there onto a sofa, but without injury. On another a weighty mahogany table near him began swaying and rocking in broad daylight. These events, and many more just as astonishing, were vouched for by men and women of impeccable reputation, and the Rev. Moses himself was universally regarded as a man of the very highest character and integrity. Trickery was inconceivable to those who knew him, and in case after case was ruled out by direct observation.

But these theatrics weren't produced for entertainment, but for the soberest of purposes: The spirits who wanted to use Moses as the medium for their message first needed to convince him they were real. Eventually they succeeded, though not without resistance by the cautious clergyman. As a result, one of the most remarkable spirit books ever written was born.

But Moses the skeptic was still concerned that what apparently came through him from spirits as he wrote automatically might in reality be nothing more than the expression of his own unconscious mind. These fears abated when he sometimes found them saying things he didn't believe. He would eventually be won over by what came through him, and underwent a kind of conversion to the spirits' beliefs, which struck him as more enlightened than what he had learned in seminary. But, as in all such spirit messages, there is no guarantee, as we saw in the Introduction, that everything the medium conveys does in fact escape the biases and predilections of the medium himself. It is worth noting that after Moses died, a spirit claiming to be Stainton Moses admitted that on several occasions he failed to convey what his spirits tried to get across through him when he was a medium. Apparently the Rev. Moses was as careful about the truth after death as he was in life!

While different spirits came through, the chief communicator called himself Imperator. Imperator identified himself as 'Imperator Servus Dei,' and said he was the chief of a group of 49 spirits. He said he came from the seventh sphere to explain the spirit world, how it is controlled, and the way in which information is conveyed to humans. As he put it, **We have before us one sole aim … we come to demonstrate to man that he is immortal, by virtue of the possession of that soul which is a spark struck off from Deity itself.**

Moses published their teachings in a book, *Spirit Teachings*, in 1883, ten years after the first messages appeared. A later book, *More Spirit Teachings*, would appear in 1892, shortly after Moses' death.

In some respects Imperator and his group were religious reformers. Sayings like the following are found throughout the book: **We call you from the dead formalism, the lifeless, loveless literalism of the past to a religion of spiritualised** truth, to the lovely symbolism of angel teaching, to the higher planes of spirit, where the material finds no place, and the formal dogmatism of the past is forever gone.

Imperator is relentless in his criticism of Victorian Christianity. He tells us that man **has perpetuated ignorant ideas about a jealous God, and a fiery hell, and a heaven in the skies where the elect are gathered, and a physical resurrection, and a universal assize [or judgment], and such notions, which belong to the age of childhood and are outgrown by the developed man. The man should put aside the notions of the child, and soar to higher knowledge.**

He tells us that the doctrine of God's authorship of the Bible is a **fable** and that distortions of the truth turn up in many places due to God's inspiration shining **through a dark medium.** He chastises the **enthusiasts** for preaching the doctrine of Jesus' atonement for our sins when dying on the cross: **The drama of Calvary was of man's not God's devising. It was not the eternal purpose of God that Jesus should die when the work of the Christ was just commencing. That was man's work, foul, evil, accursed,** not God's. As for the Resurrection, **Easter is to us the Festival of Resurrection, but not of the body. To us it symbolises not Resurrection *of* matter, but Resurrection *from* matter, the Resurrection of Spirit.** It is interesting to learn that Imperator and his group suffer because they have such limited impact on our planet when they see with such clarity where we go wrong. Chief among earth's errors is its view of God. In place of a jealous God requiring us to flatter and abase ourselves before Him, in place of **a fabled heaven, a brutal hell, and a human God,** they would have us see God as He is:

the **Supreme, All-Wise Ruler of the universe, who is enthroned over all in eternal calm, the Director and Judge of the totality of creation. ... We have not seen Him, nor do we hope yet to approach His presence. ... Ages, as you count** time, must run their course ... ere the perfected spirit – perfected through suffering and experience – can enter into the inner sanctuary to dwell in the presence of the All-pure, All-holy, All-perfect God. But though we have not yet seen Him, we know yet more and more of the fathomless perfections of His nature, through a more intimate acquaintance with His works. We know, as you cannot, the power and wisdom, the tenderness and love of the Supreme. We trace it in a thousand ways which you cannot see. We feel it in a thousand forms which never reach your lower earth. And while you, poor mortals, dogmatise as to His essential attributes, and ignorantly frame for yourselves a being like unto yourselves, we are content to feel and to know His power as the operation of a Wise and Loving and All-pervading Intelligence. His government of the universe reveals Him to us as potent, wise, and good. His dealings with ourselves we know to be tender and loving.

But *Spirit Teachings* is much more than a theological treatise. By far most of its contents deal with the nature and destiny of human beings, both here and over there. The question of struggle and suffering, briefly alluded to above, is emphasized continually. Imperator tells us, **You cannot reach the Perfect Good, save after a conflict with evil. It is an eternal necessity that you be purified through struggles with the evil that surrounds you. It is the means by which the spark once struck off from the Divine Soul wins back its way to Him and enters into its rest.** Imperator has contempt for the doctrine of easy grace. The idea that one can **wrong his neighbours, insult his God, and debase his own spirit,** yet be ushered into the very presence of God after a deathbed conversion is, according to him, ludicrous. Such a notion makes a mockery of religion. Imperator's emphasis is always on moral effort, on selfless service, on the transformation of character. There are no shortcuts to heaven – though spirit guides and guardians, God's messengers, are always available to help us on our journey.

So what actually is in store for us when we die? Strange that we even have to ask the question, Imperator tells us – so obvious is the answer:

> **As the soul lives in the earth-life, so does it go to spirit-life. Its tastes, its predilections, its habits, its antipathies, they are with it still. It is not changed save in the accident of being freed from the body. The soul that on earth has been low in taste and impure in habit does not change its nature by passing from the earth-sphere, any more than the soul that has been truthful, pure, and progressive becomes base and bad by death.**

But what is spirit-life actually like? Imperator begins to answer this question by laying out a grand map of the afterlife, with its various regions: **We believe that we state what is accurate when we say that your earth is the highest of seven spheres; that there are succeeding the earth-life seven spheres of active work, and succeeding these, seven spheres of Divine contemplation. But each sphere has many states.**

Imperator refers to the six spheres below earth as **spheres of sin,** the seven above as **spheres of work and probation,** and the highest seven as **spheres of contemplation,** for a total of 21. In some ways they are analogous to the traditional layout of hell, purgatory, and heaven, though with earth at the cusp between hell and purgatory rather than altogether off the map.

Imperator is quick to admit that he does not have any direct experience of the top seven spheres. **We are far from that blissful state,** he tells us. **We have our work yet to do; and in doing it we find our delight.** We rightly place him, as we have seen, in the topmost sphere, the seventh, of the probationary world.

On another occasion Imperator said he knew almost nothing of life in the spheres of contemplation – only what he had been told: **We only know that [a spirit] grows liker and liker to God, nearer and nearer to His image.** But about the probationary worlds – the middle kingdom, so to speak – we are told a great deal more. Once Stainton Moses went into a trance and was conducted on a tour of it:

I have no recollection of losing consciousness, but the darkness seemed to give place to a beautiful scene which gradually unfolded itself. I seemed to stand on the margin of a lake, beyond which rose a chain of hills, verdant to their tops, and shrouded in a soft haze. The atmosphere was like that of Italy, translucent and soft. The water beside which I stood was unruffled, and the sky overhead was of cloudless blue. I strolled along the margin of the lake, meditating on the beauty of the scene. I met a person coming towards me [and] knew it was Mentor [one of the group of 49 spirit communicators]. ... His voice as he addressed me was sharp and decisive in tone: 'You are in spirit-land, and we are going to show you a scene in the spheres.' He turned and walked with me along the margin of the lake till we came to a road which branched along the foot of the mountain. A little brook flowed by its side, and beyond was a lovely stretch of verdant meadow, not cut up into fields as with us, but undulating as far as the eye could reach. We approached a house, very like an Italian villa, situated in a nook, amidst a grove of trees like nothing I ever saw before; more like gigantic ferns of the most graceful and varied description. Before the door were plots of flowers of the most lovely hues and varieties. My guide motioned me to enter, and we passed into a large central hall, in the middle of which a fountain played among a bank of flowers and ferns. A delicious scent filled the air, and the sound of sweet music, soft and soothing, greeted the ear.

When Moses asked if the scene was real, Imperator said, **As real as that on which you now gaze. Your spirit was separated from its earthly body, connected only by the ray of light.**

When Moses asked if the homes of the probationary worlds were material, Imperator answered, **Yes, friend, but not as you count matter. Things are real to us, but would be imperceptible and impalpable to your rude senses. We are not fettered by space as ye are. We are free as light and air, and our homes are not localised as yours. But our surroundings are, to our refined sensations, as real as yours.**

Moses said he was astonished at how quickly the above scene unfolded. Imperator explained: **The spirit-world is around you though you see it not. Your eyes being opened, you saw the things of spirit-life, and no longer beheld the things of earth-life. ... The spirit-world extends around and about you, and interpenetrates what you call space. We wished to show you the reality of its existence.**

Imperator went on to describe the inhabitants of the first three spheres of the probationary world – the world just beyond ours:

The first three spheres are near about your earth. They are filled thus. The first with those who, from many causes, are attracted to earth. Such are they who have made little progress in the earth sphere; not the wholly bad, but the vacillating, aimless souls who have frittered away their opportunities and made no use of them. Those, again, whom the affections and affinity for pursuits of their friends restrain them from soaring, and who prefer to remain near the earth sphere, though they might progress. In addition, there are the imperfectly trained souls whose education is still young, and who are in course of elementary teaching; those who have been incarnated in imperfect bodies, and have to learn still what they should have learned on earth. Those, too, who have been prema-

turely withdrawn from earth, and, from no fault of their own, have still to learn before they can progress.

At one point Moses asked a friend of his who had recently passed (Bishop Wilberforce) if his new world was similar to earth:

> In every way similar. It is only the change of condition that makes the difference. Flowers and fruits and pleasant landscapes and animals and birds are with us as with you. Only the material conditions are changed. We do not crave for food as you, nor do we kill to live. ... We have no need of sustenance save that which we can draw in with the air we breathe. Nor are we impeded in our movements by matter as you are. We move freely and by volition. I learn by degrees and as a new-born babe, to accustom myself to the new conditions of my being. ... We can no more tell you of our life than you can convey to a deaf and dumb and blind man the true notions of your world.

Imperator added:

> Your friend gives only his impression of what he has seen in lower spheres. There spirits live in community, and are prepared under the guidance of higher Intelligences for a state of superior existence. Such spheres are states of probation and preparation, where spirits are in training for higher work. It is impossible for a spirit to be in a condition or sphere for which it is not fit.

Imperator then said: **Your friend has not left the neighbourhood, the immediate neighbourhood, of the earth. But there are similar planes, in other localities, near other planets. Spheres are conditions, and similar conditions may and do exist in many places. Space, as ye call it, is full of spirit dwellings.**

How do spirits in the probationary worlds spend their time?

> Occupations are varied. The learning and knowing more and more of the sublime truths which the Great God teaches us; the worship and adoration; the praise and glorifying of Him; the teaching to benighted ones truth and progress; the missionary work of the advanced to the struggling and feeble; the cultivation of our intellectual talents; the development of our spiritual life; progress in love and knowledge; ministrations of mercy; studies in the secret workings of the universe, and the guiding and direction of cosmic forces; in short, the satisfaction of the cravings of the immortal being in its twofold aspect of intellect and affection.

But a different kind of fate awaits those spirits who failed to better themselves on earth, who grew worse instead of better. Rector, another of the advanced spirits grouped around Imperator, explains:

> The spirit that had developed the bodily tastes, and neglected the spiritual, grows more and more earthly; the guardians are less and less able to approach it, and it gravitates further and further from light. We have said that there are six spheres below this earth [not to be understood spatially], though we have never penetrated below the fourth. Below that are the miserable, abandoned spirits who sink down deeper and deeper.

Imperator describes the fate of these debased souls in greater detail:

This tendency of bodily sin to reproduce itself is one of the most fearful and terrible of the consequences of conscious gross transgression of nature's laws. The spirit has found all its pleasure in bodily gratifications, and lo! when the body is dead, the spirit still hovers round the scene of its former gratifications, and lives over again the bodily life in vices of those whom it lures to sin. Round the gin-shops of your cities, dens of vice, haunted by miserable besotted wretches, lost to self-respect and sense of shame, hover the spirits who in the flesh were lovers of drunkenness and debauchery. They lived the drunkard's life in the body; they live it over again now, and gloat with fiendish glee over the downward course of the spirit whom they are leagued to ruin. Could you but see how in spots where the vicious congregate the dark spirits throng, you would know something of the mystery of evil. It is the influence of these debased spirits which tends so much to aggravate the difficulty of retracing lost steps, which makes the descent of Avernus [hell] so easy, the return so toilsome. The slopes of Avernus are dotted with spirits hurrying to their destruction, sinking with mad haste to ruin. Each is the centre of a knot of malignant spirits, who find their joy in wrecking souls and dragging them down to their own miserable level.

But all is not lost for these souls: In these spheres they must remain subject to the attempted influence of the missionary spirits, until the desire for progress is renewed. When the desire rises, the spirit makes its first step. It becomes amenable to holy and ennobling influence, and is tended by those pure spirits whose mission it is to tend such souls.

But great in number are the spirits who want nothing to do with purification. Imperator refers to these as **the adversaries.** Many of them get pleasure in pulling us down to their level, and their influence in our world is tremendous. To their numbers belong **the earth-bound and unprogressed spirits to whom incarnation has brought no gain, and whose affections, centred on the earth, where all their treasure is, can find no scope in the pure spiritual joys of the spheres of spirit-life.** Imperator elaborates:

> **There is direct antagonism between them and us, between the work which is for man's development and instruction, and their efforts to retard and thwart it. It is the old battle between what you call the good and the evil – between the progressive and the retrogressive. Into the ranks of that opposing army gravitate spirits of all degrees of malignity, wickedness, cunning, and deceit: those who are actively spurred on by hatred of light which an unenlightened spirit has, and those who are animated by sportiveness rather than by actual malice. It includes, in short, the undeveloped of every grade and class: spirits who are opposed, for infinitely varying reasons, to the organised attempt to lead men upward from darkness to light.**

Imperator describes the psychology of such spirits: **The spirit that has yielded to the lusts of a sensual body becomes in the end their slave. It would not be happy in the midst of purity and refinement. It would sigh for its old haunts and habits. They are of its essence.** Imperator then warns us against the modern, liberal mistake of scoffing at such notions of imperceptible evil forces bent on doing us harm: **The idea that there is no such thing as evil, no antagonism to good, no banded company of adversaries who resist progress and truth, and fight against the dissemination of what advantages humanity, is an open device of the evil ones for your bewilderment.**

Is there a head devil, a Satan, who commands the adversaries? He is an invention of **theologians,** Imperator tells us. Nevertheless, there is no lack of leadership. **Spirits, good and** bad alike, are subject to the rule of commanding Intelligences.

But let's remember that advanced spirits are constantly working to free these spirits, soul by soul, from their imprisonment in vice, and that the will is always free. Often good triumphs: **By their efforts many spirits rise, and when rescued from degradation, work out long and laborious purification in the probation spheres, where they are removed from influences for evil, and entrusted to the care of the pure and good.** Anyone who has gained sobriety through Alcoholics Anonymous can appreciate this procedure.

But are there hopeless cases? Imperator admits there are. And their destiny is tragic: **They that will not seek for anything that is good, that wallow in impurity and vice, sink lower and lower, until they lose conscious identity, and become practically extinct, so far as personal existence is concerned; so at least we believe.** Imperator calls this determined refusal to pick themselves up, this **deliberate rejection by the soul of all that is good and ennobling,** the **unpardonable sin.** But God has nothing to do with the withholding of pardon: **Unpardonable, not because the Supreme will not pardon, but because the sinner chooses it to be so. Unpardonable because pardon is impossible where sin is congenial, and penitence unfelt.** In other words, the soul chooses hell as the lesser of two evils, the greater being the arduous road to healing and regeneration. Such a soul rejects all offers of help by missionary spirits and thereby seals its own doom. Imperator tells Moses, however, that there is **no arraignment before the assembled universe ... as is in your mind. [The Day of Judgment] is an allegory. ... The soul is the arbiter of its own destiny; its own judge. This is so in all cases of progress or retrogression.** It is reassuring to be told by Imperator, **Mercifully, such cases are rare.**

What do Imperator and his friends say about reincarnation? Bear in mind that reincarnation in the late nineteenth century did not have much currency among European Christians. The idea was greeted by most Britons with incomprehension if not revulsion.

Reincarnation is certainly not prominent in *Spirit Teachings*. But it is present. Imperator says that there are times when **certain great spirits, for certain high purposes and interests, have returned to earth and lived again amongst men.** He also claims that souls lost in degradation are recycled, though not precisely as themselves. The impression one gets from a close reading is that Imperator thinks it wise to say little about the subject. Here is how he puts it:

> **There are still mysteries, we are fain to confess, into which it is not well that man should penetrate. One of such mysteries is the ultimate development and destiny of spirits. Whether in the eternal counsels of the Supreme it may be deemed well that a particular spirit should or should not be again incarnated in a material form is a question that none can answer, for none can know, not even the spirit's own guides. What is wise and well will be done. … There are other aspects of the question which, in the exercise of our discretion, we withhold; the time is not yet come for them. Spirits cannot be expected to know all abstruse mysteries, and those who profess to do so give the best proof of their falsity.**

What about the ultimate destiny of the human soul? Moses asks Imperator what happens to the spirit, long a dweller in the spheres of contemplation, who has refined away the last vestige of selfishness separating itself from the Source; and Imperator responds with modesty: **It may well be, good friend, that the noblest destiny of the perfected spirit may be union with the God into whose likeness it has grown, and whose portion of divinity, temporarily segregated during its pilgrimage, it so renders up to Him who gave it. These to us, as to you, are but speculations.**

There are millions of people in our world whose religion is based on the revelation of Imperator and his friends. Spiritualists often speak of it as their classic source. But Christians find inspiration in it as well. Imperator was merciless in pointing out the deficiencies of conventional Christianity, but his devotion to Christ and Christ's gospel of loving service pervades the work. In fact the entire book, let us recall, was motivated by a desire to serve – specifically, to turn souls away from the godless materialism sweeping across Europe and back to a confident belief in their own immortality.

We don't have space here to cover more than a fraction of Imperator's teachings. They range from the theological to the practical – from how prayer works or how to read the New Testament with its distorted record of the life of Jesus, to the proper treatment of criminals or when to end a marriage. For those who want more, both *Spirits Teachings* and *More Spirit Teachings* are available free online. One particularly helpful website, www.geocities.com/spirit_teachings/, even organizes the teachings by topic.

Chapter 2

The Afterlife of a Young Texan

From my experience I have learned that the spirit world is around us, that our spirit friends are with us every day, and that there is a tie which binds their hearts to ours so that they are with us many times and try to make us feel their presence.
Alice Stringfellow

Leslie Stringfellow died in his hometown of Galveston, Texas, in 1886 after a brief illness. He was 20 years old. His father, Henry, was a prominent horticulturalist and his mother a pianist. Leslie himself was a gifted musician doted on by both parents, especially his mother, Alice. He was an only child. Alice was devastated by his death and out of desperation sought to make contact with him using a planchette. She would describe the process many years later:

I was told to place my hand lightly on [the planchette] and await results. This I did for many days in vain until one day I suggested that my husband put the tips of his fingers on one end while I lightly placed mine on the other. The results were marvelous. Writing came, so legible and plain, and each day there were written pages and pages. Neither my husband nor myself could write without the other so we made an appointment for every evening at the same hour when our little table and planchette would be ready, with large sheets of white paper. And no one knows our joy and happiness when our boy told us ... all about his friends and companions and pastimes there. He said that he was our same boy, that he was happy to be with us and to make himself known and that my perseverance had accomplished this happiness.

Leslie communicated to his parents in this manner for the next 15 years, but it wasn't until another quarter century passed, and after Sir Arthur Conan Doyle (the creator of Sherlock Holmes, and student of mediumistic literature) encouraged publication, that Alice at last decided to publish selections from Leslie's letters. She published a mere 100 copies for distribution to family and friends. Her selections for the book were a small fraction of Leslie's complete opus. She found countless instances of evidential and had no doubt about the identity of the author.

Leslie's Letter to His Mother was lost to the world until a librarian at the University of Arkansas, Stephen Chism, stumbled across a copy and was so intrigued by it that he undertook to bring it out in a new edition (2005) with the title *The Afterlife of Leslie Stringfellow*. I worked with both the original edition and Chism's beautifully edited version.

One of the book's most remarkable features is Leslie's description of his world's geographic relation to ours. In agreement with all other accounts we've read, his world is physically close to our own, though in a different dimension. But Leslie is more specific than other spirit communicators. He tells us that **the spirit world begins very near the earth and extends millions of miles beyond. It surrounds yours on all sides, like the atmosphere does the globe, and every nation has its counterpart in spirit, surrounding it, in connection with that part over or nearest its earthly place of residence.** In other words, most Hindus live in the part of the spirit world that hovers over India, and most Chinese over China. And, as we've seen, each region extends indefinitely outward. Further, **There is a spiritual sun which shines through yours, and lights our world. Our sun shines always, but for few hours out of each 24 is not as bright, and that is our night, from about your 12 p.m. to about 5 a.m.** This description tallies with our reality. Leslie's night would be shorter than ours because, since he dwells farther out from the earth's surface, the earth would block out the sun less completely during the spirit world's night. A good geometer could use this information to locate Leslie's approximate distance from the earth's surface. As for the weather, Leslie tells us the temperature is always pleasant, as it is on a mild summer day. It never rains, but there are **gentle mists about every two weeks.** Spiritualists sometimes use the word 'Summerland' to describe the region where spirits neither habitually good or bad, as well as children, find themselves after death. From now on we'll use this word for Leslie's world.

In keeping with this designation, Summerland is enchant-ingly beautiful. Gorgeous trees and flowers, shady glades and rushing streams, towering mountains and sparkling lakes, striking land features and charming little villages, vast oceans with islands, and large cities – all of these are here. And there are animals, plenty of them. Leslie speaks of a vast forest set apart for wild animals where one may visit without fear of harm. He visited this place and saw **great monsters that lived thousands of years before man came.** Another part of Summerland was a kind of bird sanctuary:

> **This is a part of the world for all wild water fowls that lived on earth. You cannot conceive the countless millions of ducks, geese and that class of fowls. Some flew away but many times they just swam off and seemed to watch us with great curiosity. There were low trees and on one side a vast rocky cliff on which were curious looking birds that lived on earth before men.**

Of special interest is his claim that our earth is a gestation ground for all the species of flora and fauna that he finds in his world, and that men and women have been developing Summerland for thousands of years just as they've been devel-oping earth. In other words, Summerland is not ready-made by God, but has been developed into an ever more splendid world system over the centuries by our ancestors. This claim is borne out by references to Summerland's cities and technology, which are 'engineered' by spirits out of astral matter. One day Leslie went with his friends

> to the Mountain of Fine Arts. It is situated many thousands of miles from here and this was the first time we had been there. The whole mountain is a grove of grand trees and at intervals on the sides are situated the most magnificent temples or halls you can conceive. One is dedicated to Music, one to Painting, one to Sculpture, one to Machinery, and other things, and on the top was a great temple of the Poets. ... I spent a good part of the day in the Hall of Music and heard Mozart lecture on the 'Theory and Science of Music.'

Another time he watched a new drama by Shakespeare in the Hall of Poetry:

> This Hall is fitted up with a stage and is one of the most beautifully decorated buildings here. The seats are all covered with the finest damask and the ceiling is one grand fresco, painted by Michael Angelo [sic]. There were more than one hundred artists and the principal part was acted by Garrick. You know there is a universal spirit language and though all the poets and artists of different countries were there, of course they could all understand.

But not all was art for Leslie. He tells us that one day he **went to our Atlanta – each community and country in your world has its counterpart all around it in [ours] – and met Jefferson Davis, president of the Confederacy during the Civil War.** Another time he heard Benjamin Franklin deliver a lecture on electricity. Leslie traveled widely and rewarded his curiosity every chance he had. But Socrates, he tells us, was out of reach:

> **Socrates is with the advanced spirits, way up in the spheres. We cannot go there, only know that it is a very lovely world. They come to us to teach and inspire, by what you would call scientific philosophy. Progression to the higher spheres depends greatly upon the desire of each person, and also upon the effort to acquire knowledge. ... The higher one goes the more elevated he is in knowledge and goodness. We are satisfied in this, the second sphere [Summerland], and must stay here as long as we are satisfied.**

We should not forget that Leslie was only 20 when he died and that his interests in Summerland would have corresponded to his age. And in fact Leslie has what we would call a great deal of fun. In addition to music lessons under the spirit world's best violinists, he traveled all over his world, sometimes walking, sometimes moving **by will-power.** He thoroughly enjoyed these trips. On one occasion he discovered **an immense lily of the Victoria Nyanza variety** in the center of a large lake near his grandmother's home:

> **It is the most enormous thing you can imagine and yet the most beautiful. The leaves float on the surface and are as large as this room, and very thick. I walked all over one leaf. In the center of the plant are seven enormous flowers, as white as snow, shaped like a morning glory, with scalloped edges. One was leaning over on its side, and I got in it, and was hidden from view.**

And Leslie went to parties. **Nothing gives us more fun than when a party of young folk get together and relate their earth experiences.** On December 20, 1889, he told his parents how he and friends planned a Christmas party for some of

Summerland's orphaned children. They planned to select a fir tree and materialize **all kinds of jewels and gifts and toys** to decorate it with. When the children arrive, **I am to hide in the tree and when all are assembled will play on my violin a Christmas piece which I composed.** On December 25 he described the festivities to his parents: **The children all stood around and sang beautiful Christmas hymns, and when all the presents were off the tree, we dematerialized it, and it melted away into a green vapor, and disappeared.**

But all is not fun and games in Summerland. Even though Leslie describes it as **a thousand times better in every way** than our world, he later admitted that his mother's depression following his death – a depression that stretched out for eleven years – **has many times been bitterness to me.** Other spirits suffer from neglect. They want to be remembered, to be in their loved ones' thoughts, to have even a single flower left on their gravestone. Loneliness can figure prominently in Summerland. At one point Leslie makes a plea to all of us on earth to make more use of the medium's gift. If we did, if we kept up a running conversation with 'the dead,' fewer of them would be so soon forgotten.

Then there is 'the Realm of the Unprogressed,' a euphemism for hell. There are many different levels in this realm, but we have space to view only one, a sub-world for the most debased among us. Alice occasionally received messages from others besides Leslie, and in this case it was her cousin Bettie who came through. This is how she describes the inhabitants: **They are what you would call the scum of the earth and have passed their lives in vice and crime. There is but one such place for this class, but its extent is incredible and its population immense. They live in discord and misery and everything is dark and forbidding, and a dull leaden fog pervades the air at all times.** Bettie tells Alice that she sometimes enters their world to help them out of their predicament – for no one is damned eternally by an angry God. Such visits are common: **Every good spirit who has friends there goes often to see them and makes every effort to awaken in them sorrow for their past lives and a desire for the purer and higher life.** But such efforts are usually

> a thankless task, for many of them are so wedded to their terrible life that they actually take pleasure in it, and resist every effort that is made in their behalf. But some see their error and are brought to feel the wrong of such a life, and embrace the first opportunity to escape. They have no settled occupation, but live in idleness and it is sad to think how many, by their lives on earth, are preparing a residence for themselves in this dreadful place.

A poignant communication came to Alice on one occasion from an old school chum who had become addicted to morphine:

> My dear Alice:
> I am so unhappy over the bad life of my poor child [back on earth]. She is a slave of the awful drug that ruined me. Yes, and my heart aches for Helen's future. I have repented but that does not save her from the consequences of my bad example.
> I have been here [in Alice's upstairs parlor where the planchette is located] many times and it gives us great relief to be able to confess our wrongs to you. I never saw Leslie, for he is far happier than I am [and lives in a different zone of the afterworld].
> Mary Martin

It would be natural for some readers to wonder if all believers in a non-Christian religion find themselves in the Realm of the Unprogressed. Leslie tells us this is decidedly not so and shows a remarkable knowledge of non-Christian faiths for his time. You will remember that the adventurous Leslie and his friends are fond of travel. Here is what he says about the Chinese:

> The Chinese people resemble very much their earthly bodies and their faces have the same almond eyes and flat noses, and they dress for all the world like they did on earth. In fact, I believe every nation, when its people first pass over, keeps the same characteristics that marked them on earth. When spirits from any part of our world go to some other they are recognized at once as strangers and every possible attention is shown. We received any number of invitations to spend the day and were shown around by gentlemen wherever we wanted to go.

Many a Westerner who has heard classical Chinese music will understand Leslie's reaction to it the first time he heard it: **Of all the hideous groaning and growling and creaking, you never heard the like. And just to show how people's tastes differ, I looked around after the overture was concluded, and the whole crowd were in a broad grin of delight and were applauding for all they were worth.**

It's clear from Leslie's many visits to Summerland's various realms that (1) no one race or religion is favored over another, and that (2) people prefer to live among others of similar background and culture, just as they do here on earth. Of Hindu India, for example, he says, **This part of the Spirit World is very exclusive and those who live here seldom go elsewhere.**

If right belief isn't the determinant of salvation, then what is? The answer is clear from the first page: **True religion is to love God who is our father, and do all we can to make others happy.** By God, Leslie does not have in mind a purely conventional notion. He tells us **that God dwells in the trees and flowers as well as in us, and that the entire world in all its forms is but an expression of His life and power.** Without being in the least preachy, Leslie tells his mother, **I did not appreciate the beauty of an unselfish life on earth as I should have done, for oh, Mamma, there is no happiness so pure as that which flows from helping others, no matter how humble or small the favor done may be. Heaven would be on earth, if only that spirit prevailed.** People aren't saved by their theology or by what scripture they follow. They advance themselves by their growing knowledge and their willingness to serve others in love. Faith in God is reflected everywhere in this account, but Leslie makes it clear that loving actions are the gunpowder of spiritual progress. Those actions are sometimes directed at us, with everything from a labor-saving invention to a great musical idea to a more inclusive spirituality being telepathically impressed by spirits on the most receptive and fertile earth minds for the good of the planet.

Nevertheless, Summerland is not a Communion of Saints. The best Summerlanders are spirits in progress, like Leslie. Many grades of progress are described, and even a spirit's home **is an index of his character.** Great spirits are not to be found here, unless they be teachers come down for a spell from a higher sphere.

Summerland is also, as mentioned above, a place for children. And there are millions of them, most of them orphans. Leslie comes close to being an orphan himself – not because his parents have died before him, but because he has died before them. But he is already a young man, not a child. Let's look briefly at the life of orphans in Summerland:

There are many homes for children here, and today we visited one situated in an immense grove of trees and the buildings covered a space of ground as large as a small town.

This was for small children under seven and eight years. Older ones have other homes, where they go after leaving

these infant ones.

The children are watched over and cared for by the most beautiful and motherly spirits who in their earth-life were especially fond of children. These are entirely orphans, as we call them, or children whose parents are still on earth, but who will take them home when they themselves come over.

These children are educated in every branch of knowledge and those who have special tastes for music, painting and other accomplishments are given every opportunity to cultivate these talents.

In talking to these little ones, it was easy to tell those who had had no earthlife or experience. They seemed more spiritual, but not so sympathetic and affectionate, as the others who had known a mother's love on earth.

Not in this whole Spirit World is there a child who would for a moment think of wishing to leave this bright and happy home, in exchange for the pains and sorrows of your world.

On one occasion Leslie and his friends attended a school outing. Sitting under trees, they delighted in telling the kids stories of earth:

I told them all about the overflow in Galveston in 1886, when I went down and got the ducks. And about the snakes, about my boat, and the pears, and what astonished them most was that you raised pears 'to sell.' These had not known earth-life, and here, as you know, all is gift. And when we told them money was little round pieces of metal, they could not understand why anyone wanted it, and we had to laugh at their curious questions.

We will leave you with a thought that doesn't fit in with anything else we've discussed here. Leslie tells his mother and father that he's been **reading an old book that tells all about the earth as it was 20,000 years ago and about the lost continent of Atlantis.** He tells them that

> **it extends from the Azore Islands, which are the tops of its mountains, to nearly across the Atlantic Ocean. It was a highly civilized and densely peopled country, with great cities and beautiful and fertile lands and for thousands of years was the home of the arts and sciences. ... This beautiful country through the settling of the interior of the earth suffered an earthquake in the middle of the night, and in a few moments was engulfed and lost from sight.**

This account squares with research-based theories that have surfaced recently in our own time, though, of course, no one really knows.

Most of the classic nineteenth-century accounts of the next world come to us from advanced spirits, such as we found in the preceding chapter. What distinguishes this account is its exuberant boyishness. Leslie is no sage or philosopher, just a well-brought-up, fun-loving, but thoroughly intelligent young man from Texas. His experiences vary from theirs accordingly.

Chapter 3

A Notable American's First Year on the Other Side

If one demands to know what purpose there is in life, tell him that it is this very evolution of the Master out of the man. Eternity is long. The goal is ahead for each unit of sufficient strength, and those who cannot lead can serve.
Judge David Hatch

A eulogy in the February 21, 1912 edition of the *Los Angeles Times* described Judge David Hatch, the spirit communicator featured in this chapter, as 'a great man.' He was certainly remarkable. After serving for seven years as an elected judge of the superior court of Santa Barbara County, he resigned to practice law in Los Angeles, then eleven years later retired again to study spiritual philosophy, write fiction, and think about life's ultimate meaning and purpose. During this period he lived as a hermit in the mountains of British Columbia. He resumed his law practice five years later.

The medium is a woman named Elsa Barker who shared Hatch's interests in spirituality. They were friends for six years up to his death. She wrote prolifically over an eleven-year period between 1904 and 1915, including a play and books of poetry and fiction. Three of her works during this period were produced automatically, two coming from Judge Hatch, and the third, a book of poetry, from one of the characters we will be meeting here, the so-called 'Beautiful Being.'

Of all the books written automatically that I've read, the Hatch/Barker collaboration, titled *Letters from the Afterlife*, has the greatest stylistic beauty. Perhaps in part for this reason, the strangeness of Hatch's world almost slaps one in the face. The big themes are identical to those we see in other books from this genre, but the details of his account are fresh, sometimes bizarre, sometimes mysterious – rather like what you would expect of a world you had never set foot in.

Hatch's first communication came while Barker was living in Paris and before she even knew he was dead. After a letter reached her a few days later telling her of his death, she experimented to see if he would come again. He did. He would come for the next eleven months. She described their collaboration: 'While writing these letters I was generally in a state of semi-consciousness, so that, until I read the message over afterwards, I had only a vague idea of what it contained. In a few instances I was so near unconsciousness that as I laid down the pencil, I had not the remotest idea of what I had written; but this did not often happen.' Barker left out nothing from Hatch 'except personal references to [his] private affairs, to mine, and to those of his friends.' In these excluded writings she sometimes found references 'to past events and to possessions of which I had no knowledge, and these references were verified.' She also tells us that Hatch 'made a few statements relative to the future life which are directly contrary to the opinions which I have always held.' This evidential material made a strong impression on her and left no doubt in her mind that it was really her friend coming through her and not some ideas tucked away in her subconscious. It also removed any fear of death she had. In one of his earliest appearances, he writes through her: **After years enough he [the soul] grows weary of the material struggle [on earth]; his energy is exhausted. He sinks back into the arms of the unseen, and men say again with bated breath that he is dead. But he is not dead. He has only returned whence he came.**

One of the more intriguing themes of the book is the ordinariness of most spirits. You might think that death would call them to their senses and unleash spiritual energy that would lead to a quest for enlightenment. In several places Hatch laments that this is not so: **This is not a place where everyone knows everything – far from it. Most souls are nearly as blind as they were in life.** Elsewhere he says, **I am sorry to say that the person who has a clear idea of the significance of life is about as rare here as on the earth. ... a man does not suddenly become all-wise by changing the texture of his body.** Or again:

> **This is a great place in which to grow, if one really wants to grow; though few persons take advantage of its possibilities. Most are content to assimilate the experiences they had on earth ... most souls do not demand enough here, any more than they did in life. Tell them to demand more, and the demand will be answered.**

He gives an example:

> **I have often been sorry for men who in life had been slaves of the business routine. Many of them cannot get away from it for a long time; and instead of enjoying themselves here, they go back and forth to and from the scenes of their old labors, working over and over some problem in tactics or finance until they are almost as weary as when they 'died.'**

On the other hand, he describes other spirits who are more ambitious. Teachers and schools abound, and they exist to help anyone who will listen. Hatch's own teacher, like others, 'works for the work's sake, and not for reward or praise.' Hatch tells a touching story about his teacher:

> **He is very fond of children, and one day when I was sitting unseen in the house of a friend of mine on earth, and the little son of the house fell down and hurt himself and wept**

bitterly, my great teacher, whom I have seen command 'legions of angels,' bent down in his tenuous [invisible] form ... and soothed and comforted the child.

Not only are there teachers in Hatch's world, teachers both for us on earth and those who have passed; there are 'Messiahs' or 'Christs.' Teachers – Hatch himself sees himself as a novice teacher – work one-on-one with strong souls **ambitious for growth,** but Messiahs have a different task:

The weak [souls] are the charges of the Messiahs and their followers. But, nevertheless, between us and the Messiahs there is brotherhood and mutual understanding. Each works in his own field. The Messiahs help the many; we help the few. Their reward in love is greater than ours; but we do not work for reward any more than they do. Each follows the law of his being.

And there are even gods. Hatch explains:

I have been told that there are also planetary beings, planetary gods ... the guardian spirit of this planet Earth evolved himself into a god of tremendous power and responsibility in bygone cycles of existence. ... What do you fancy will be the gods of the future cycles of existence: Will they not be those who in this cycle of planetary life have raised themselves above the mortal? Will they not be the strongest and the most sublime among present spirits of men? Even the gods must have their resting period, and those in office now would doubtless wish to be supplanted. To those men who are ambitious for growth, the doors of development are always open.

But don't imagine that these 'future gods' come from the rich and famous of earth. **That a soul had houses, lands, and honors among men does not increase his value in our eyes,** Hatch tells us. **On earth you value titles, inherited or acquired; here a man's name is not of much importance even to himself, and a visiting-card would be lost through the cracks in the floor of heaven. No footman angel would ever deliver it to his Lord and Master.**

Hatch is fortunate enough to befriend a spirit he calls simply the **Beautiful Being.** One chapter is given over to a poem that this **amazing angel** wrote for him:

> **What earthly father can escape his children? What earthly mother wishes to?**
> **But I! I can make a rose to bloom – then leave it for another to enjoy.**
> **My joy was in the making. It would be dull for me to stay with a rose until its petals fell.**
> **The artist who can forget his past creations may create greater and greater things.**
> **The joy is in the doing, not in the holding fast to that which is done.**
> **Oh, the magic of letting go! It is the magic of the gods.**

The Beautiful Being, who is sexless, enthralls Hatch. At one point he can only cry out, **You irresistible one! Who are you? *What* are you? ... I love you with an incomprehensible love.** One night the Beautiful Being takes Hatch on a journey:

> **When, on my voyage that night with the Beautiful Being, I had feasted my eyes upon beauty until they were weary, my companion led me to scenes on the earth which, had I beheld them alone, would have made me very sad. But no one can be sad when the Beautiful Being is near. That is the**

charm of that marvelous entity; to be in its presence is to taste the joys of immortal life.

Hatch says that this being **has changed my ideas about the whole universe: ... everything may take its proper place in the infinite plan, of which even your troubles and perplexities are parts, inevitable and beautiful.**

Hatch's account is remarkable for other reasons. One is the sheer scope of the worlds he introduces us to: a **pattern world** that is the basis of our earth, various heavens, **many hells ... mostly of our own making,** faraway planets populated by **a race of beings wonderful to behold,** even the Catholic's purgatory. To begin with, Hatch corroborates the claim of Leslie Stringfellow in the preceding chapter: **You and the solid earth are in the center of our sphere,** he tells Barker. He later tells her that souls, **when they come out [die], usually remain in the neighborhood where they have lived, unless there is some strong reason to the contrary.** So we embodied beings share space with the world of spirits, unseen by us though they are; and we tend to stay in the countries and among the people we are familiar with – again just as Stringfellow told us.

One of Hatch's major themes is the interest that spirits have in us. They are attracted to us when we **are laboring under some intense emotion, be it love or hate, or anger, or any other excitement.** Have you ever seen someone become so furious that he did not seem himself? Anger is especially magnetic to a certain class of **inimical spirits. ... A small seed of anger in your heart they feed and inflame by the hatred in their own. It is not necessarily hatred of you as an individual; often they have no personal interest in you; but for the purpose of gratifying their hostile passion they will attach themselves to you temporarily.** Lust and avarice are just as apt to attract the wrong kind of spirit.

As for hell, Hatch does not describe it as a single place where sinners are lumped together. Instead, there are hells to fit every vice: hells of lust, of avarice, of hatred, of untruthfulness, of anger, of various addictions. But these hells, though full of suffering, are not punitive; rather they exist for spirits who *want to be there* and who want to express themselves in the sick ways they used to back on earth. Often they do so at our expense. Hatch describes a scene at a bar:

> A young man with restless eyes and a troubled face ... was leaning on the bar, drinking a glass of some soul-destroying compound. And close to him, taller than he and bending over him, with its repulsive, bloated, ghastly face pressed close to his, as if to smell his whiskey-tainted breath, was one of the most horrible astral beings I have seen in this world since I came out. The hands of the creature ... were clutching the young man's form, one long and naked arm was around his shoulders, the other around his hips. It was literally sucking the liquor-soaked life of its victim, absorbing him, using him, in the successful attempt to enjoy vicariously the passion which death had intensified.
>
> But was that a creature in hell? you ask. Yes, for I could look into its mind and see its sufferings. For ever (the words 'for ever' may be used of that which seems endless) this entity was doomed to crave and crave and never to be satisfied.
>
> And the young man who leaned on the bar in that gilded palace of gin was filled with a nameless horror and sought to leave the place; but the arms of the thing that was now his master clutched him tighter and tighter, the sodden, vaporous cheek was pressed closer to his, the desire of the vampire creature aroused an answering desire in its victim, and the young man demanded another glass.

It would be wrong to think that suffering is restricted to spirits residing in their self-made hells. As on earth, decent individuals sometimes disagree. And Hatch, a judge and something of a sage back on earth, **is called upon here to decide matters for others.** On one occasion a man asked for help resolving the following dilemma:

> **There are two women here who in life were married to one man, though not at the same time. The first woman died, then the man married again, and soon – not more than a year or two later – the man and his second wife both came out [died]. The first wife considers herself the man's only wife, and she follows him about everywhere. She says he promised to meet her in heaven. He is more inclined to the second wife, though he still feels affection for Wife No. 1. He is rather impatient with what he calls her unreasonableness. He told me one day that he would gladly give them both up, if he could be left in peace to carry out certain studies in which he is interested.**

The dilemma is never resolved, and Hatch finds himself wondering if the only way the man **can get free from his two insistent companions is by going back to the earth.**

Which brings up reincarnation, a subject Hatch likes to philosophize on. The following is typical:

> **You should get away from the mental habit of regarding your present life as the only one, get rid of the idea that the life you expect to lead on this side, after your death, is to be an endless existence in one state. You could no more endure such an endless existence in the subtle matter [of Hatch's world] than you could endure to live forever in the gross matter in which you are now encased. You would weary of it. You could not support it.**

Yet Hatch does not look forward to another life on earth. In one of the book's more memorable passages, he tells us,

What strange experiences one has out here. I rather dread to
go back into the world [earth], where it will be so dull for
me for a long time. Can I exchange this freedom and vivid
life for a long period of somnolence [in the womb], afterwards to suck a bottle and learn the multiplication tables
and Greek and Latin verbs? I suppose I must – but not yet.

When, then? Hatch has thought a lot about this:

I could probably force the coming back [to earth], but that
would be unwise, for I should then come back with less
power than I want. ... it is better for me to rest in the
condition of light matter until I have accumulated energy
enough to come back with power. I shall not do, however, as
many souls do; they stay out here until they are as tired of
this world as they formerly were tired of the earth, and then
are driven back half unconsciously by the irresistible force
of the tide of rhythm. I want to guide that rhythm.

What does he mean by having **less power than I want?** He
explains: ... **when the soul enters matter, preparing for rebirth,
it enters potentiality, if we may use such a term, and all its
strength is needed in the herculean effort to form the new body
and adjust to it.**

If we ask of Hatch what the connection is between a soul
**coming out into the sunlight of another life on earth [and] the
details of his former experience,** he explains that, although
specific memories are not usually recalled, **the tendencies of any
given life, the unexplained impulses and desires, are in nearly
all cases brought over.** This, incidentally, is the position held by
Hindus and Buddhists.

But Hatch's philosophy is not particularly Eastern. It's true
that he warns his readers not to make the mistake of coming over
with a mind set against reincarnation. He tells us that many such

minds do not realize they can reincarnate even *after* they come over, so adamant is their resistance to the possibility. But he has visited **one of the highest Christian heavens** and speaks glowingly of it. He has even seen the one **called the Savior of men, and last night I saw Him in all his beauty.** Hatch does not regard Jesus as God or the unique savior of the world, but as **the paradigm of the spiritual man: Jesus is a type of the greatest Master. He is revered in all the heavens. He grasped the Law and dared to live it, to exemplify it. And when He said, 'The Father and I are one,' he pointed the way by which other men may realize mastership in themselves.** Jesus, like other Masters, represents the highest ideal: **If one demands to know what purpose there is in life, tell him that it is this very evolution of the Master out of the man. Eternity is long. The goal is ahead for each unit of sufficient strength, and those who cannot lead can serve.**

There is much about Hatch's message to us that is purely informative, not profound or inspiring. Did you ever wonder if astral bodies breathed? They do. In another place he tells us he **met a charming woman the other night. ... She was no less a woman because she weighed perhaps a milligram instead of one hundred and thirty pounds.** As for creature comforts, **We are no longer bothered by hunger and thirst; though I, for instance, still stay myself with a little nourishment, an infinitesimal amount compared with the beefsteak dinners which I used to eat.** Regarding movement, **Why, it takes more energy on earth to put one heavy foot before another heavy foot, and to propel the hundred or two-hundred pound body a mile, than it takes here to go around the world!** Regarding the arts, **I think the happiest people I have met on this side have been the painters. Our matter is so light and subtle, and so easily handled, that it falls readily into the forms of imagination. There are beautiful pictures here.** Regarding homebuilding, **The soul in the 'hereafter' builds its own house, and the** materials thereof are free as air. If I use the house which another has built, I miss the enjoyment of creating my own. And there are hobbies, knitting being one of them. **Do not be shocked. Did you fancy that a lifelong habit could be laid aside in a moment?** As for souls who died as children, **There are no violent changes. The little ones grow up ... about as gradually and imperceptibly as they would have grown on earth. The tendency is to fulfill the normal rhythm, though there are instances where the soul goes back very soon, with little rest. That would be a soul with great curiosity and strong desires.** Such a soul had attached himself to Hatch and called him Father. The boy, named Lionel, had died six years before at the age of seven, and now he was eager to go back to earth. He had even elected his mother-to-be, a woman **who had always been good to him** and was a friend of his former mother. He wanted to become an engineer, and Hatch's reaction is interesting: **It is strange about this boy. Out in this world there is boundless opportunity to work in subtle matter, opportunity to invent and experiment; yet he wants to get his hands on iron and steel. Strange!**

But is it really? Months later, in his last communication, in early 1913, Hatch wrote the following:

> **The joy of the struggle! ... Remember that your opponents are not other men, but conditions. If you fight men, they will fight you back; but if you fight conditions, they, being unintelligent, will yield to you with just enough resistance to keep your muscles in good order. ... Whatever your strength, make the most of it in the challenge of life.**

Lionel wanted to go back to earth because he sought a greater challenge than the astral world provided. Presumably, if Hatch's view of things is right, that's why most of us are here now: to **enjoy difficulties as a swimmer enjoys the resistance of water.**

Hatch's world is full of characters from a great variety of conditions. As for Hatch himself, he comes across as insatiably curious and well-roundedly human. **I have made wonderful discoveries in the archives of my own soul,** he tells us. **There I have found the memories of all my past, back to a time almost unbelievably distant.** Yet he misses his loved ones: **... the call of earth is loud sometimes, and my heart answers from this side of the veil.** He takes leave of Ms. Barker, and us, with an announcement that he's **going out with the Beautiful Being on a voyage of discovery... to see faraway planets and meet their inhabitants.** *Bon voyage,* Judge Hatch!

Chapter 4

A Psychical Researcher on This Side Speaks to Us from the Other Side

... a stupendous vision of the progression of the human spirit through eternity ...
Nandor Fodor

The medium Geraldine Cummins was an Irish woman who authored 22 books, 15 of them automatically while in a light trance. She described her method in this way:

> I am a mere listener, and through my stillness and passivity I lend my aid to the stranger [spirit] who is speaking. It is hard to put such a psychological condition into words. I have the consciousness that my brain is being used by a stranger all the time. It is just as if an endless telegram is being tapped out on it. The great speed of the writing suggests actual dictation, as though some already prepared essay were being read out to my brain.

E. B. Gibbes, a member of the Society for Psychical Research who sat beside her and assisted her for years as she channeled many different personalities, vouched that Cummins wrote in 50 different handwritings, none her own, each belonging to a different spirit. Often she produced the psychological idiosyncrasies of characters she had never met but were verified as authentic by those attending the seance. She wrote at tremendous speed, very unlike her sluggish pace when writing consciously. She was one of the most gifted mediums of the twentieth century.

The spirit communicator, Frederic Myers, was trained in the classics, lectured for a time at Trinity College Cambridge, wrote some very fine poetry, and spent the last thirty years of his life as a school inspector and advocate of women's higher education. But it was during that last period, after meeting Stainton Moses in 1874, that his life's true vocation surfaced. He would become to psychical research what Freud was to psychotherapy. One of the co-founders of the Society for Psychical Research in 1882, his influence on the young movement was immense. His monumental book *Human Personality and Its Survival of Bodily Death* is still regarded by many as the greatest work on psychical research ever to appear.

More to the point for our purposes, he was one of the spirits that came through Cummins. He first spoke through her in 1924, 23 years after his death, and reappeared intermittently until 1931. (He also communicated through other mediums from time to time.) The book we'll be examining here, *The Road to Immortality*, is the record of their collaboration. It combines very fine writing with a rare breadth of vision.

Before looking at the world that emerges in this book, it's worth noting that the spirit claiming to be Myers expresses impatience with the English language as well as with mediums who sometimes find it hard to blank out their own minds' contents. Much about the world he tries to describe, especially the last three of the seven planes, can only be approximated by our language. It is with a feeling of awe, even unworthiness, that I try to summarize his account of these realms. In places the language becomes fuzzy, virtually unintelligible, so far beyond the world we are familiar with is his subject. One can imagine his impatience!

But he does manage to get across with clarity what it feels like, from his side, to work through a medium as gifted as Cummins. Here is what he said, writing through her hand, early in their partnership:

The inner mind [of the medium] is very difficult to deal with from this side. We impress it with our message. We never impress the brain of the medium directly. That is out of the question. But the inner mind receives our message and sends it on to the brain. The brain is a mere mechanism. ... In other words, we send the thoughts and the words usually in which they must be framed, but the actual letters or spelling of the words are drawn from the medium's memory. Sometimes we only send the thoughts and the medium's unconscious mind clothes them in words.

Myers makes it clear that he is far from infallible, even though he's been in the spirit world longer than most communicators and has some experience of higher planes. But even at his level there is much that is mysterious, and spirits sometimes disagree with each other, he tells us, just as we do on earth.

He begins by announcing that there are seven planes that spirits journey through, the first being a physical planet like our earth. It is followed by

(2) Hades or the Intermediate State.
(3) The Plane of Illusion.
(4) The Plane of Colour.
(5) The Plane of Flame.
(6) The Plane of Light.
(7) Out Yonder, Timelessness.

Myers has little to say about Hades, that place situated **on the frontiers of two lives, on the borders of two worlds.** For him it was a resting place, a kind of hospice where he recovered his strength and prepared himself for entry into the great world beyond. **Pray do not conjure up unpleasant associations with Hades,** he tells us. **I died in Italy, a land I loved, and I was very weary at the time of my passing. For me Hades was a place of** rest, a place of half-lights and drowsy peace.

Myers doesn't tell us what happened to him next, but it's clear he spent most of his time in the third and fourth planes. We'll examine each in turn.

Think back to Leslie Stringfellow's pleasant environment, which he referred to as Summerland. Myers uses the same word to name the Third Plane, but more often he calls it, as we have just seen, the 'Plane of Illusion.' He also calls it the 'Memory-world.' Each of these terms brings out an important aspect of the Third Plane. Myers leads us into this world with these opening remarks: When people die,

> **They hunger for the dream which was home to them ... they enter into a dream that, in its main particulars, resembles the earth. But now this dream is memory and, for a time, they live within it. All those activities that made up their previous life are re-enacted, that is, if such is their will ... the soul, freed from the limitations of the flesh, has far greater mental powers, and can adapt the memory-world to his taste. He does so unconsciously, instinctively choosing the old pleasures, but closing the door to the old pains. He lives for a while in this beatific, infantile state. But, like the baby, he inhabits only a dream, and has no knowledge and hardly any perception of the greater life in which he is now planted [the Fourth Plane].**

Myers does not mean it is a literal dream, or a subjective illusion like a mirage, but only that it is a distraction or diversion from important business, and that it **fades before spiritual knowledge.** In fact Myers likens it to **the fundamental unreality of earth,** which of course, as we know, is real enough for us. A more helpful metaphor might be Disneyland. Disneyland is a real place, but it is also a place of pleasant, idealized make-believe, certainly not a part of the natural world. In the same way, the Third Plane that will greet us when we die will have been constructed by spirit architects who have the wisdom to know what we need at our present stage and the power to construct it.

Myers invents a typical character named Tom Jones to make his point. Jones, an ordinary lawyer's clerk living in London all his life, has now just died and finds himself

> **born into the next world with all his limitations, with all his narrowness of outlook, with his affections and his dislikes. ... He bears within him the capacity for recalling the whole of his earth life. Familiar surroundings are his desperate need. He does not want a jeweled city, or some monstrous vision of infinity. He craves only for the homely landscape he used to know. He will not find it here in the concrete sense, but he will find, if he so desires, the illusion ... It undoubtedly presents a more attractive appearance than his little grey London world, but in essentials it is of the same familiar stuff from which his England is made.**

He will also **find his friends, some of his own people, and those two or three persons he really loved; that is, if they have already gone [died] before him, been summoned by death at an earlier time.** He tells us, **'Nearly every soul lives for at time in the state of illusion.'**

For most of us the Third Plane will be pleasant and familiar. Tom Jones's environment won't look much like a typical Eskimo's, but both will be free of suffering. There are exceptions, however. For example,

> **The cruel man who has changed his natural craving for affection into a longing to give pain to others necessarily finds himself in a world here where he cannot satisfy this craving. ... In the new life [following death] he has not, for**

a time at any rate, the power to inflict pain on anything living. This means for him, with his greatly increased mental powers, a very terrible distress. ... The misery of such an unsatisfied state is largely of a mental character. What use to him is a world of light and beauty while still this foul earth longing is unsatisfied?

Myers uses another example to show the great variety of experience in this 'Illusion Land.' He asks us to consider the plight of a man who chased women and lived for sex. He finds,

when he enters the Kingdom of the Mind, that as his mental perceptions are sharpened so his predominant earth-desire is intensified, his mental power being far more considerable. He can, at will, summon to himself those who will gratify this over-developed side of his nature. Others of his kind gravitate to him. And for a time these beings live in a sex paradise. ... They yearn still for gross sensation, not for that finer life, which is the spirit of sexual love, that perfect comradeship without the gratification of the grosser feelings. They obtain it in abundance, and there follows a horrible satiety. They come to loathe what they can obtain in excess and with ease; and then they find it extraordinarily difficult to escape from those who share these pleasures with them.

But eventually they will escape – Tom Jones from his unchallenging London-look-alike world, and the sex partners from each other. But what then? Where do they go next? It all depends, says Myers. It depends on how spiritually evolved they are. Broadly speaking, every human being falls under one of three headings. He or she is either **Spirit-man, Soul-man, or Animal-man.** The Animal-man, probably a majority of the human race during any time period, lives for pleasure. He doesn't care for the joys of the intellect or the fine arts. He doesn't read good literature. His appetites are exclusively physical and, as Myers puts it, **paltry.** There is no danger he will have gotten this far in our book. He is probably not cruel or corrupt; he might be sweet and generous. But his mind and spirit are still slumbering. And when he grows tired of the unchallenging look-alike world of the Third Plane, he desires change:

> **Usually, at this point, when longing for a new life with all his being, he desires that it shall be one with the flesh, that it shall be another episode passed in the grosser bodily forms. So he goes downwards; but he descends in order to rise. ... During his next incarnation he will probably either enter into the state of the Soul-man, or he will at least be less of an animal, and will seek an existence and follow a life of a higher order than the one he led when previously lodged in the flesh.**

On the other hand, **I am told that the Animal-man occasionally prefers to enter a material existence on some other planet in which matter may be even denser than any earthly substance.**

But the Soul-man, as opposed to the Animal-man, when finally bored of the Third Plane, will embark on a very different kind of experience. He or she is now **an intelligent, ethically developed soul** and will elect to go upward to the next level, the Fourth, not downward for a repeat performance on a dense planet.

On the Third level, where familiarity and comfort had the highest priority, one's 'astral' body was usually a replica of one's earth body. Not on the Fourth. Here the Soul-man dons a 'subtle body,' a body entirely dissimilar from the human body. As regards appearance, it can only be described as being apparently a compound of light and colours unimaginable. The shape of this form is influenced by all the ego's past acts so far as they have impressed themselves on his deeper consciousness. This coloured compound may be grotesque, bizarre in form, may be lovely beyond words, may possess strange absurdities of outline, or may transcend the loftiest dream of earthly beauty. ... It is far more fluidic, less apparently solid than earth surroundings.

And the outer environment of the Fourth Plane is compatible with his body:

Within the subtle world of which I speak you will perceive a variety of forms which are not known on earth and therefore may not be expressed in words. Yet there is a certain similarity, a correspondence between the appearances on this luminiferous plane. Flowers are there; but these are in shapes unknown to you, exquisite in colour, radiant with light. Such colours, such lights are not contained within any earthly octave, are expressed by us in thoughts and not in words. For, as I previously remarked, words are for us obsolete. However, the soul, in this plane of consciousness, must struggle and labour, know sorrow but not earth sorrow, know ecstasy but not earth ecstasy. The sorrow is of a spiritual character, the ecstasy is of a spiritual kind.

Unlike the pleasant, insouciant, 'illusory' Third Plane of relatively low vibration, this **many-coloured world is nourished by light and life in a greater purity [and] vibrates at an unimaginable speed.** This higher vibration hides it from earth's most sensitive instruments, but in spite of its invisibility there is nothing remotely illusory about it. The Soul-man's sensitivity has also been stepped up. Everything is experienced more intensely with his super-ethereal body and his IQ of 500. However, this heightening of experience doesn't lead only to heavenly bliss, but sometimes to intense suffering, as when one meets an old enemy. His hatred of you will hit **your body of light and colour** like a withering blast; for **the old emotional memory will awaken when you meet,** and it will not be dimmed down by the sluggish earth brain you used to labor through. Myers puts it this way:

> **You will understand, therefore, that pain and pleasure, joy and despair are once more experienced. Again, however, they differ greatly from the earthly conception of them; they are of a finer quality, of an intellectualized character. Mightier is their inspiration, more profound the despair they arouse, inconceivable the bliss they stir within the deeps of your being.**
> **On this luminiferous plane the struggle increases in intensity, the efforts expended are beyond the measure of earthly experience. But the results of such labour, of such intellectualised and spiritualised toil and battle also transcend the most superb emotion in the life of man. In brief, all experience is refined, heightened, intensified, and the actual zest of living is increased immeasurably.**

Myers goes on to say that on the Fourth Plane **the soul wears several bodies, passing from one to another as he advances** and that the **thought processes of the emotional life seem limitless when compared with the sluggish movements of the human brain.** Sublime exaltation, titanic struggle, acute suffering, indescribable bliss, and a thrilling sense of no-nonsense realness – all this and much more will comprise the future of those of us who resist the allure of another incarnation on earth. So reports Frederic Myers from the Other Side.

Before passing on to a description of the remaining three planes, Myers introduces us to the Group Soul, one of the hallmarks of the Fourth Plane. A Group Soul is **a number of souls all bound together by one spirit.** There are countless Group Souls, each headed and inspired by a single spirit of uncommon power. Each Group Soul might contain as few as 20 souls or as many as a thousand. And there is some unifying interest, for example music, that acts as the thread that binds the group together. Not all groups, however, are conducive to the growth of the souls that make it up. Although every soul is free, **a fanatical Buddhist or a very devout Christian may be held within the groove of his earthly beliefs** as if **held in chains,** and **such conditions tend to inhibit progress.** But most Group Souls significantly quicken progress. Myers is himself a member of one: **The interesting feature of my state here is that I am within a larger mind, and many of my affinities are contained in it.** He tells us we will **realize how fine and beautiful is this brotherhood within the one being; how it deepens and intensifies existence; how it destroys the cold selfishness so necessary to an earth life.**

Of special interest is the economy of the Group Soul. Each soul is so privy to the experiences of its fellows that the lessons normally learned only by a succession of many reincarnations can be speeded up. It works like this:

> **... what the Buddhists would call the karma I had brought with me from a previous life is, very frequently, not that of my life, but of the life of the soul [in my group] that preceded me by many years on earth and left for me a pattern which made my life. I, too, wove a pattern for another of my group during my earthly career. We are all of us distinct, though we are influenced by others of our community on the various planes of being.**

Myers tells us he will not reincarnate. The surrogate experiences of his brothers and sisters, which he feels with as much intensity as if he were the actor, are teaching him all the remaining lessons of earth needed for his advancement.

That brings us to the Fifth Plane, the so-called Plane of Flame. Myers does not dwell at this level, so his description comes across as second-hand and vague. Added to that, this plane **may be imagined but not understood or conceived by a man's mind.** We are in rarified air here. Myers tells us that an inhabitant here **remains himself, yet is all those other selves [in his group] as well. He no longer dwells in form – as it is conceived by man – but he dwells still in what might be described as an 'outline' … an outline of emotional thought: a great fire which stirs and moves this mighty being.** Such a being **is continuously conscious. … He tastes of Heaven and yet the revelation of the last mystery tarries, still awaits the completion of the design of which he is a part.**

The Sixth Plane is even more nebulous. The bodies of spirits at this level are formless white light, and **pure reason reigns supreme. Emotion and passion, as known to men, are absent. White light represents the perfect equanimity of pure thought. Such equanimity becomes the possession of the souls who enter this last rich kingdom of experience. … They are capable of living now … as the pure thought of their Creator. They have joined the Immortals.**

The Seventh (and last) Plane – which Myers refers to simply as **Out Yonder** – is the end game, the **final purpose,** and no longer counts as a realm of creaturely experience. Without a body of any kind, you merge with the **Great Source** and reign **in the great calm of eternity. Yet you still exist as an individual [and] are wholly aware of the imagination of God. So you are aware of the whole history of the earth from Alpha to Omega. Equally all planetary existence is yours. Everything created is contained within that imagination, and you … know it and hold it.** An eon of spiritual evolution is usually required before taking this final step: **Only a very few pass out Yonder during the life of the earth. A certain number of souls attain to the sixth state, but remain in it or, in exceptional cases for a lofty purpose, descend again into matter. They are not strong enough to make the great leap into timelessness, they are not yet perfect.**

Myers' vision of our place in this stupendous scheme of things is both humbling and exhilarating. We are such puny creatures, yet our potential is unlimited. Apparently the Great Source has ambitious plans for us! Anyone looking for an easy ride into Eternal Life is in for a severe shock if Myers is correct.

What exactly is the Infinite's plan for us? Myers states it early on:

The purpose of existence may be summed up in a phrase – the evolution of mind in matter that varies in degree and kind – so that mind develops through manifestation, and in an ever-expanding universe ever increases in power and gains thereby the true conception of reality. The myriad thoughts of God, those spirits which inform with life all material forms, are the lowest manifestation of God, and must learn to become God-like – to become an effective part of the Whole.

All this sounds impossibly lofty. How can such words mean much to us – to us who run on such low spiritual octane, us kindergarteners? We feel a queasiness in our stomachs! Yet the last words that Myers leaves us with are as down-to-earth as you can get: **Happiness comes through effort; through a wise and controlled indulgence in the pleasures of the senses; through athletic activities for the perfecting of the body; through study for the development of the mind; and through toleration of a charitable outlook. The development of these leads to the culti-vation of the spirit.** He even recommends making a good salary:

A desire for money in moderation is a virtue, for it happens to be a desire to become a complete man, and, through such completion and its resultant content, to benefit others. And who can deny his rapport with the common man or woman with this down-home reference: **I have been changing, evolving, putting on, if you will, like the trees, a fresh coat of leaves, but unchanged within; so that my wife and my children will know me [when they die] though some of my earth memories be buried as the foliage underground when winter comes.**

In the final analysis, however, Myers' account stands out for many of us as one of the most fertile after-death communications in the entire literature because of its soaring vision of what our future can hold. The stunted being that we are now will bear little likeness to the colossus we will become – if we are willing to work for it.

Chapter 5

A Catholic Priest Describes the 'Land of the Great Harvest'

The day will assuredly come when our two worlds will be closely interrelated, when communication between the two will be a commonplace of life, and then the great wealth of resources of the spirit world will be open to the earth world, to draw upon for the benefit of the whole human race.
Monsignor Robert Hugh Benson

Robert Hugh Benson, the communicator of this work, was born in 1871 the son of Edward White Benson, the Archbishop of Canterbury. The younger Benson was ordained to the Anglican priesthood in 1901, but converted to Roman Catholicism three years later. In 1911 he became privy chamberlain to Pope St. Pius X and managed the pope's household and appointments. He was solidly identified with the Catholic world.

During his short life – he died in 1914 – he became famous in England and America for several novels, especially *The Necromancers* (1909), in which he ridiculed and condemned spirit communication as 'dealings with the devil.' After his death he would be haunted by a need to atone for the mistake he made in this novel. It was not until much later, however, that he was permitted by his spirit advisors to correct it. *Life in the World Unseen*, first published in 1954, is now in its thirteenth printing. In this book Benson, speaking through the medium Anthony Borgia, tells us he was psychically gifted while functioning as a Catholic priest, but was taught by the Church to think of the gift as a **mental aberration.** He confesses: **To have followed my own** inclinations would have entailed a complete upheaval in my life, a renunciation of orthodoxy, and most probably a great material sacrifice, since I had established a second reputation as a writer. ... The truth was within my grasp, and I let it fall. His regret would launch one of his tasks after passing: **What I wanted was to try to undo something that I wished I had never done. ... What I had written I could never unwrite, but I could ease my mind by telling the truth, as I now know it, to those who were still on the earth-plane.**

Anthony Borgia was a clairaudient medium: he heard a voice, inaudible to anyone else, that identified itself as coming from Benson. Monsignor Benson had known Borgia when Borgia was only a child. Borgia was only thirteen when Benson died, but Borgia always remembered the older man's attentions with affection and reverence. *Life in the World Unseen* was one of several books clairaudiently dictated by Benson. (It is available online for free.) Borgia died in 1989 at the age of 93.

Besides his desire to set the record straight regarding spirit communication, Benson had two other motives for communicating. First, he wanted to show that the doctrines and scriptures of Christianity, and of all other religions, were, in spite of their pretensions, wholly man-made and often dead wrong. After having passed,

> **I could see volumes of orthodox teachings, creeds, and doctrines melting away because they are of no account, because they are not true, and because they have no application whatever to the eternal world of spirit and to the great Creator and Upholder of it. I could see clearly now what I had seen but hazily before, that orthodoxy is man-made, but that the universe is God-given.**

Feasts like Epiphany (the three wise men's visit to the baby Jesus) and Pentecost (the Holy Spirit's descent upon the Apostles) have

very little moment here. Only Christmas and Easter are widely celebrated, but they are reinterpreted. They are timed to synchronize with earth's celebrations, but they apply to everybody, not only to Jesus: **Both Christmas and Easter are looked upon as birthdays: the first, a birth into the earth world; the second, a birth into the spirit world.**

His second motive was to remove a near-universal misapprehension among Christians concerning the actual nature of the afterlife. Near the end of his book he writes: **I hope that, by now, I have sufficiently indicated that the spirit world is not a land of idleness, not a land where its inhabitants spend the whole of their lives in a super-ecstatic atmosphere of religious exercises, formally offering up 'prayer and praise' to the Great Throne in a never-ceasing flow.** The world he describes is a diviner world than ours by far, but it is also a world we would feel at home in. This is the world we will be looking at for the rest of the chapter.

Of all the accounts I've read, this one goes into the greatest detail about what I might call the *physics* of the world to come. One chapter is devoted to time and space as they are perceived by spirits. Another deals with the geographical position of the spirit world relative to earth. After telling us that the earth world and the spirit world **interpenetrate one another,** and that the **low realms of darkness are situated close to the earth-plane,** Benson explains more fully: **With the spirit world made up of a series of concentric circles, having the earth world approximately at the centre, we find that the spheres are subdivided laterally to correspond broadly with the various nations of the earth, each subdivision being situated immediately over its kindred nation.** The careful reader might recall that this description coincides exactly with Leslie Stringfellow's account in Chapter 2.

Another section of the book is devoted to the flowers of the spirit world, still another to the soil. Yes, the soil! The following paragraph is typical:

To obtain an adequate idea of the ground upon which we walk and on which our houses and buildings are erected, you must clear your mind of all mundane conceptions. First of all, we have no roads as they are known on earth. We have broad, extensive thoroughfares in our cities and elsewhere, but they are not paved with a composite substance to give them hardness and durability for the passage of a constant stream of traffic. We have no traffic, and our roads are covered with the thickest and greenest grass, as soft to the feet as a bed of fresh moss. It is on these that we walk. The grass never grows beyond the condition of being well-trimmed, and yet it is living grass. It is always retained at the same serviceable level, perfect to walk upon and perfect in appearance.

Benson tells us there are many 'realms' or 'spheres' within the spirit world. He lives in a happy realm, a kind of paradise of forests and meadows, of seas and lakes, of warm breezes and lovely birdsong, of cloudless clear light emanating from the central sun. Many inhabitants are homeless, for homes are not needed: there are no thieves or bad weather in Benson's realm. Nevertheless, many spirits choose out of habit to live in houses dotting the countryside, while others cluster together in cities.

Benson takes us to the seashore at one point:

The view was simply magnificent. Never had I expected to behold a sea. Its colouring was the most perfect reflection of the blue of the sky above, but in addition it reflected a myriad rainbow tints in every little wavelet. The surface of the water was calm, but this calmness by no means implies that the water was lifeless. There is no such thing as lifeless or stagnant water here. From where we were, I could see islands of some considerable size in the distance – islands that looked most attractive and must certainly be visited!

Beneath us was a fine stretch of beach upon which we could see people seated at the water's edge – but there was no suggestion of overcrowding! And floating upon this superb sea, some close at hand – others standing a little way out, were the most beautiful boats.

He also found splendid cities in the spirit world. He describes one of them:

As we approached the city, it was possible for us to gather some idea of its extensive proportions. It was, I hardly need to say, totally unlike anything I had yet seen. It consisted of a large number of stately buildings each of which was surrounded with magnificent gardens and trees, with here and there pools of glittering water, clear as crystal. ... Here we find broad thoroughfares of emerald green lawns in perfect cultivation, radiating, like the spokes of a wheel, from a central building which, as we could see, was the hub of the whole city. There was a great shaft of pure light descending upon the dome of this building, and we felt instinctively ... that in this temple we could together send up our thanks to the Great Source of all.

But there were more important things to do than sightsee. Learning is a passion for Benson, for the pursuit of truth leads to progress upward into higher worlds and thus greater happiness. Learning meant, for Benson, spending a lot of time in the city's immense 'hall of literature.' This library was unlike earth's in more ways than its size. He explains:

I have dipped into history, and I was amazed when I started to read. ... I found that side by side with statements of pure fact of every act by persons of historical note, by statesmen in whose hands was the government of their countries, by

65

kings who were at the head of those same countries, side by side with such statements was the blunt naked truth of each and every motive governing or underlying their numerous acts – the truth beyond disputation. Many of such motives were elevated; many, many of them were utterly base.

Another way to grow in spirit is by serving others. Benson tells us he is governed by a **constant urge to be doing something useful. Something that will be of benefit to others.**

But all is not work. Much of the time work and play are intertwined, as in theatrical productions. Comedies usually center on the predicaments and misadventures of the old earth life: **We can go to see comedies where, I do assure you, the laughter is invariably much more hearty and voluminous than is ever to be heard in a theatre of the earth-plane. In the spirit world we can afford to laugh at much that we once, when incarnate, treated with deadly seriousness and earnestness!** Historical pageants are even more interesting, especially when the actors are the very men and women who played those roles back on earth: **But surely the most impressive, and, at the same time, interesting experience is to be present at one of these pageants where the *original participants* themselves re-enact the events in which they were concerned, first as the events were popularly thought to have occurred, and then as they actually took place.** In still other ways spirit theater is different from ours. For example, **In such pageants the coarser, depraved and debased incidents are omitted entirely, because they would be distasteful to the audience, and, indeed, to all in this realm. Nor are we shown scenes which are, in the main incidents, nothing but battle and bloodshed and violence.**

It is interesting to see what Benson says about the sports of earth. In the spirit world thought controls movement, and the usual effects of gravity can be annulled at will. Therefore **anything in the nature of propelling a ball by striking it would**

lead to quite hopeless results. Lest anyone should be saddened at the prospect of there being no baseball or cricket to while away the hours, Benson says, **There is such a superabundant supply of vastly more entertaining things to be seen and done here, beside which a great deal of the earthly recreations appear sheer trivialities.**

There is a whole chapter on occupations and jobs, others on the arts. Much work as we know it on earth does not exist. In a world in which there is no garbage, no dust, no industrial waste, no heating or cooling, no bodily illness, no way to physically injure oneself or another, and no difficulty getting from one place to another, that is not surprising. There are no cars, no felling of forests, no laundries, no appliances, no emergency rooms, no meds to remember to take, no bomb factories, no banks, and no stock exchanges. Harmony reigns to such an extent that there aren't even any trial lawyers! Benson mentions a small orchard and even eats one of its delicious fruits, but nothing like agriculture exists. There is an immense amount of teaching, counseling, building, gardening, craftsmanship, and artistic expression. Music is the supreme art form, and craftsmen are needed to make the instruments. Libraries abound, and books have to be printed. Tapestries need to be woven. (Not cloth for clothing, because clothing is part of a spirit's body.) Cities have to be built. So there are plenty of jobs to do: **All that we have in our halls and our houses, in our homes and in our gardens, has to be made, to be fashioned, or created, and it requires someone to do it. The need is constant, and the supply is constant, and it will ever be so.** In one fascinating chapter he describes in detail how a building is constructed – quite a contrast to the way we do it! The only rule concerning occupations in the spirit world is that you don't have to do a job you dislike because you need the money.

In perhaps the most surprising pages of the book, Benson tells us that sound and light are intimately connected in the spirit world – so much so that, as he puts it, **all music is colour, and all colour is music. The one is never existent without the other. That is why the flowers give forth such pleasant tones when they are approached. ... The water that sparkles and flashes colours is also creating musical sounds of purity and beauty.** Since light and sound are always found together, is it possible to control light in the process of making music? It is, and **musical architecture** is the result. We see an example of this in an open-air concert that Benson attended: **The musical sounds sent up by the orchestra were creating, up above their heads, this immense musical thought-form, and the shape and perfection of this form rested entirely upon the purity of the musical sounds [and] the purity of the harmonies.**

A composer, we are told, **can build a majestic form as grand as a Gothic cathedral.** Benson was tremendously excited by the experience: **Unlike the earth where music can only be heard, there we had both heard and *seen* it.**

You might think there is no place for science in the spirit world, but this is not so. Scientists are plentiful, and much of their time is spent trying to understand better the incredibly complex laws of their own new world. Others seek to transmit (telepathically) to earth the discoveries they have made that will help it. Benson claims that **the earth world has the spirit world to thank for all the major scientific discoveries that have been made throughout the centuries.** In fact the spirit world is far ahead of earth, so far that certain discoveries are withheld until a time that they would not be **misused by unscrupulous people.**

So what is Benson's occupation? He functions as neither scientist nor artist. Instead he plays the role of the priestly counselor – a role he enjoyed back on earth and enjoys again. But the aim of the counseling is peculiar to the spirit world. He explains:

The percentage is low, deplorably low, of people who come into the spirit world with any knowledge at all of their new life and of the spirit world in general. All the countless souls without this knowledge have to be taken care of, and helped in their difficulties and perplexities. That is the principal work upon which Edwin, Ruth [his closest friends] and I are engaged. It is a type of work that appeals to many of the ministers of the church of whatever denomination. Their experience upon earth stands them in good stead, and all of them – perhaps I should say all of *us!* – know that we are now members of one ministry, with one purpose, serving one cause, and all of us possessed of the same knowledge of the truth of spirit life, without creed, without doctrine or dogma, a united body of workers, men and women.

One of the most respected occupations is that of the spirit guide; each of us on earth has one or more, and they are often behind the subtle promptings to virtue that we sometimes act on. This is what Benson says about this class of spirit:

Spirit guides constitute one of the grandest orders in the whole organization and administration of the spirit world. They inhabit a realm of their own, and they have all lived for many centuries in the spirit world. ... It would be safe to say that by far the greater number of spirit guides carry on their work all unknown to those whom they serve, and their task is so much the heavier and more difficult. ... It naturally saddens them to see the mistakes and follies into which their charges are plunging themselves, and to be obliged to stand aloof because of the thick wall of material impenetrability which they have built up round themselves. ... Inspiration, devoted to whatever cause or pursuit, comes from the world of spirit, and from nowhere else.

Benson goes on to say that without the constant influence of spirit guides

> the earth would, in a very brief time, be reduced to a state of complete and absolute barbarity and chaos. And the reason is that man thinks he can get along nicely by his own powers and volition. He is conceited enough to think that he requires no help from any source whatever ... your world looks very dark to us, and we try very hard to bring a little light to it. We try to make our presence known, our influence felt.

Many other spirits are engaged in what I've called in previous chapters missionary work; out of compassion they feel called to descend into the dark regions of the spirit world, spirit regions very close to earth, and lead lost souls out of their misery.

The missionary spirit must first cross a boundary. On one occasion, under the guidance of an experienced spirit, Benson and his friends walk (they *choose* to walk rather than teleport) into a country that is desert-like:

> We saw no flowers, no trees, no dwellings, and everywhere seemed bleak and barren. There was no sign of human life, and life seemed to be rapidly disappearing from beneath our feet, as by now the grass had ceased altogether, and we were upon hard ground. We noticed, too, that the temperature had fallen considerably. Gone was all that beautiful, genial warmth.

It would get worse. As they progressed, they eventually came upon the inhabitants of this dark, chilly world – many of them. There would be no devil, as in Dante, and no damnation by a righteous God. Instead,

> We could see, as we walked along, whole bands of
> seemingly demented souls passing on their way. ... Their
> bodies presented the outward appearance of the most
> hideous and repulsive malformations and distortions, the
> absolute reflection of their evil minds. ... The multi-
> tudinous sounds that we heard were in keeping with the
> awful surroundings, from mad raucous laughter to the
> shriek of some soul in torment – torment inflicted by others
> as bad as himself.

Eventually they came upon a region whose inhabitants looked
subhuman, a place where **all manner of bestialities and
grossness, and such barbarities and cruelties as the mind can
scarcely contemplate** were seen. One man in particular fasci-
nated them. He showed **not the least sign of regret for his
loathsome earthly life ... we could not feel one tiny vestige of
sympathy for this inhuman monster.** Yet even for him there was
hope: ... **we could do nothing but hope that one day this
dreadful being would call for help in true earnestness and
sincerity. His call would be answered – unfailingly.**

If this sounds stark, it is. Benson does not find a God who
magically transforms such persons into saints by divine fiat.
Benson's God does not alter human character, because to do that
would be the same as destroying one person and replacing him
with another. Instead he finds a law of karma at work everywhere, a law of the deed that governs the destiny of every spirit.
Benson puts it this way:

> **Perspectives and view-points are completely altered when
> one comes into the spirit world. However mighty we were
> upon the earth-plane, it is spiritual worth only that takes us
> to our right place in the spirit world, and it is the deeds of
> our life, regardless of social position, that at our transition
> will assign to us our proper abode. Position is forgotten, but**

deeds and thoughts are the witnesses for or against us, and we become our own judges.

Not only do people's deeds, or rather their character molded by those deeds, determine which of the many realms they land in; it determines the very house they are assigned:

An indispensable prerequisite to the ownership of a spirit home is the *right* to own it, a right which is gained solely by the kind of life we live when incarnate, or by our spiritual progression after our transition to the spirit world. Once we have earned that right there is nothing to prevent our having such a residence if we should wish for one.

In the meantime spirits must be content to stay where they belong, almost always somewhere between realms **infinitely better [than theirs] – and others infinitely worse.** And that is as it should be. Benson and his friends, for example, do not envy those more evolved spirits who live in **realms of surpassing beauty** that they can't reach, but look forward to the time that they **have earned the right to enter, either as visitors or as inhabitants.** As for boundaries between realms, **Each sphere is completely invisible to the inhabitants of the spheres below it, and in this respect, at least, it provides its own boundary.** In other words, just as we cannot see the spirit world all around us because it is too ethereal for our gross senses to pick up, so spirits belonging to lower spheres, such as newcomers like Benson, cannot see more refined spheres that belong to more refined souls.

We have looked at the dark regions where souls stubbornly unrepentant dwell, but what about those regions that are heavenly? Benson devotes a long chapter to **the highest realms.** He tells how he and his friends were invited by one of the great souls residing there for a visit. To get there, they had to pass through many realls, for they **were about to be taken into realms far, far removed from [their] own normal habitation.** Their guides took extraordinary measures to adjust the visitors' vision **to the extra intensity of light** of the high world they would be entering. I do not have space to describe much of what they saw. Here are Benson's opening words: **We were in a dominion of unparalleled beauty. There is no imagination upon the earth-plane that can visualize such inexpressible beauty, and I can only give you some meager details of what we saw in the limited terms of the earth-plane.** He goes on to describe

> an unending vista spread before us of more earthly miles than it is possible to contemplate. And all through this wide expanse we could see other magnificent buildings built of still more precious stones – of emerald and amethyst, to name but two, and, far away, what looked like pearl. Each of the different buildings was set amid the most entrancing richness of colour and grandeur of form. Wherever we cast our eyes, there we could see the flashing of jeweled buildings, reflecting back the rays of the central sun, the myriad colours from the flowers, and the scintillations from the waters of the river that flowed before us far away into the distance.

But it was the people they met that charmed them the most. They **were greeted by the most friendly and gracious beings, who thus added to our welcome. Welcome, indeed, was the overmastering feeling that enveloped us.** Eventually their host explained why they had been invited:

> to show that the inhabitants of such high realms are not shadowy unreal people, but, on the contrary, they are like ourselves, capable of feeling and exhibiting the emotions of

their fine natures, capable of human understanding, of human thought, and as easily susceptible to laughter and free-hearted merriment as were we ourselves ... and that although it may take countless years of time to reach those realms, yet there is all eternity in which to achieve that end, and that there are unlimited means to help us upon our way.

The spirit world according to Benson is a place of endless variety spread out in virtually infinite space – with every individual spirit residing in a realm suitable to his or her spiritual maturity. It is indeed, as the title of this chapter suggests, **the land of the great harvest.**

There is much more in the Borgia/Benson collaboration that we don't have space for. A whole chapter on organization and leadership would interest any student of management. Another chapter, devoted to children, backs up what Leslie Stringfellow told us in Chapter 2. In several places Benson refers to the **old earthly religion** that is still practiced: **The same ceremonies, the same ritual, the same old beliefs, all are being carried on with the same misplaced zeal – in churches erected for the purpose.** One final point is worth mentioning. Unlike many other channeled communications I've read, there is not a word about reincarnation in the whole book, and it is clear that Benson, if we take him at his word, expects to spend the rest of eternity in the spirit world. He doesn't even see the need for infants or babies born dead to try again. He tells us that what we call death is just **the casting off of the physical body ... whether infants or aged ... and entering, for all time, the world of spirit.**

We will come back to the puzzling questions raised by divergent views on reincarnation in the final chapter.

Chapter 6

Oh, the People We Meet Over There!

Never have we read such a spontaneous, simple, direct, happy and instructive series of scripts from 'the other side.'
Science of Thought Review

In December 1965, a month after her death, Frances Banks, an Anglican nun for 25 years, found a 'pure, unobstructed channel' through which to describe the bracing new world she found herself in. The 'channel' was the mind of her close friend Helen Greaves. Greaves tells us what it felt like when Frances came through: 'Gently, imperceptibly, I became aware of Frances. She was influencing my mind and, quite distinctly, I "registered" the thoughts she was conveying to me. Indeed, as soon as I let myself "listen" the thoughts formed into words and without a moment's hesitation I reached for my pen.'

Thus was born *Testimony of Light*, a this-world/next-world collaboration between two highly respected elderly Englishwomen. In a preface to the book, Anglican Canon J. D. Pearce-Higgins ranks *Testimony of Light* with Mother Julian of Norwich's Christian classic *Revelations of Divine Love*. I agree with the ranking, but the comparison is in other respects misleading. *Testimony* is not a book from medieval Europe, and many a Christian would find it heretical in several places. On the other hand, the spiritual and moral life urged on the reader is entirely consistent with the gospel of love and forgiveness preached by Jesus – or indeed by the saints and sages of the world's major religions.

Without further ado, let's dive in.

Upon 'coming over,' Frances finds herself in a 'kind of rest home' run by the nuns of her order. **I am now lying in a bed, high up on a terrace, that looks over a vast sunlit plain. It is a beautiful scene, and so restful. ... I am recuperating from the illness [cancer] which brought disintegration to my physical body.**

A few days later she was attracted to Exeter Cathedral where a memorial service for her was underway. This was her first descent, or visit, to earth following her death. Communicating through Greaves, she wrote, **I longed to materialize before you to show there is no death; but that was beyond my power to do.**

She apparently underestimated her abilities, for several in the small crowd later testified they saw her ghost dressed in the nun's habit she wore while incarnate. A powerful personality in life – her friends said she had a 'will of iron' and was 'fearless and outspoken' – the intensity of her spirit seemed to break through the veil dividing the worlds.

Frances quickly recuperated and was up and about. She tells us: **I am now occupying a 'cottage' of my own ... with a very pretty garden ... bright with golden flowers.**

It isn't long before she draws conclusions about her strange, yet familiar, new world: **I kept assuring myself in wonder, 'I have made The Change!' I realized then that I could both see and hear as before, only now in a more *intense* way.**

She elaborates: **'So this is death!' I recall saying to one of the Sisters who was beside me – *'Life separated by density* – that is all!'**

One of her earliest experiences is also one of the most fascinating. Many of us were taught as children to think of Judgment Day as a frightening ordeal. There we are, worried and skulking, bent low before the God of the Universe who, sitting on a throne surrounded by angels, is preparing to judge us and send us to heaven, hell, or purgatory. But that's not at all the way it is, says Frances:

Somewhere in the deeps of my mind two 'blueprints' are brought forward into my consciousness. These are so clear that I can (literally) take them out, materialize them and study them. One is the Perfect Idea with which my spirit went bravely into incarnation. The other is the resultant of only a partially-understood Plan ... in fact my life as it was actually lived. ... First of all the mind looks at the whole comparison, and sets the blueprints side by side. This is the first shock; a true humbling of yourself to find that you did so little when you would have done so much; that you went wrong so often when you were sure that you were right. During this experience the whole cycle of your life-term unfolds before you in a kaleidoscopic series of pictures. During the crisis one seems to be entirely *alone*. Yours is the judgment. You stand at your own bar of judgment. You make your own decisions. You take your own blame. ... You are the accused, the judge and the jury.

Judgment – the logic behind it, the way it plays out in individual cases – is the leading theme of this book. Its midsection focuses on sixteen spirits Frances met. She tells us about their earth lives, then shows us what awaits them in the afterlife. We are introduced to a Nazi leader **lodged in the shadows** for 20 years since his suicide in 1945, and a young Jewish mother **bound to him by her deep hatred.** The Shadowlands are of special interest to Frances. She tells us there are **hells of the spirit and the mind, confining states of misery; dark, depressing and as real as the tortured consciousness of the dweller therein makes them. ...** [They contain] squalid dwellings inhabited by unhappy, tormented beings who jeer and mock and pursue their warped existences.

At one point she, along with three of her fellow nuns and several protective guardian spirits, entered one of these regions and talked at length with a French painter **reduced to the gutter** shortly before his violent death. There he was, painting. His smelly hovel was stacked with paintings: **They were all the same; all dark, all hideous, all primitive and almost evil in their sardonically clever interpretation of character and all exceedingly ugly. But there was one strange feature common to all of them. A door … its dark panels closing away a suggestion of light.** She talks to him:

'You're making your own hell, you know.'
He swept out his arm in an eloquent gesture. '*I never made this.*'
'Not actually, only by your thoughts you have … just as the others have done.'
'The others here? … Haven't an idea in their heads. They don't even know the differences between light and shade. …'
'And do you?' I pointed deliberately to the masses of dingy colour in his picture.
His temper rose at once.
'Yes, I do!' he roared. He stalked across the room, back to his easel, glared at the half-finished canvas on it. 'Damn your eyes. I could paint once. I *did* paint I tell you, really paint. …'
'But not now?'
Suddenly he was quiet, anger spent. 'Could *you* paint here?' he whispered.

The conversation continues until Frances, with assistance from one of her companions, convinces him to try introducing light into his pictures. Amazed at the turn of events, he allows himself to leave the dingy street he lives on and walk up **towards a hill where the gloom was threaded with a spear of brightness.** This story underscores the point that no one, however corrupt, is hopelessly lost, no one is condemned to hell forever. Frances tells us that missionary spirits routinely ply these dark spaces and invite **the stumblers** to turn their backs on their crimes and receive rehabilitation. The French painter is typical. He might not find comfort in the light the first time he's led out of the murk, but the next time might be easier. No one, however, is ever forced. C. S. Lewis said that 'the gates of hell are locked from the inside.' Strange to say, many are the spirits who, after a lifetime of evildoing, feel more at home inside the gate, inside their self-made hell, as far away from the light as they can get. Frances tells us there are three conditions to be met before there can be progress: facing one's defects, yearning to be free from those defects, and service to fellow spirits. Some want to change, some don't. Just as on earth.

We've been looking at the dark side of the afterlife, but there is much more light than darkness in Frances's book. One of the spirits she tells us about

> had been a nurse and missionary for many years of her life in Africa, and had *lived* the Christian religion. She was put to death when there had been an uprising by the natives, and with her, a small native boy whom she had befriended. They had arrived here together, for it seemed that even in the period of transition to this plane she had held the child to her with love.

This humble woman lacked a **well-developed intellect [but] radiated peace and love and joy; and death had meant little to her.** As a result, she was translated to her rightful place in one of the **Higher Spheres.**

Seventeen months after Frances's death, Frances herself had made progress. Helen Greaves, the medium, reports having a vision of Frances, and this vision tells us as much about the world to come as Frances's words. This is what Greaves saw:

I had a distinct 'vision' of Frances. This was not the Frances I had known, nor was it the Spirit I had 'seen' clairvoyantly in her habit when she was present at her own Memorial Service. ...This was a different Being, a Spirit filled with Light, radiant and glorious. ... I distinctly recall that her robe impressed me. It was of a light soft blue and it sparkled and shone. ... Her face was the face of a young woman. She looked breathtakingly beautiful.

Stagnation in self-made hells of the Lower Astral. Progress upward to a Higher Sphere where dwell great souls and teachers of wisdom. Each of these destinies, one upward and the other downward, is self-made. But there is a third destiny, and now we must turn to it.

The most captivating segment of the book tells of a girl named Jeannie who wanted more than anything to become a dancer but contracted polio at the age of eight. After months in an iron lung, she came out with one leg shrunken and shorter than the other. When she died of pneumonia three years later, she woke up in the care of the sisters, Frances among them. Frances and Jeannie became fast friends.

Jeannie didn't at first understand that she had died, so it was with speechless wonder that she saw her legs:

She ran her hands up and down her calves, over the ankles, fingering the bones of the feet carefully and then back to the knees. She did this over and over as if she couldn't believe that which she could feel and see. She was silent, puzzled. It evidently never occurred to her to stand up. Habit was still too strong. She just sat there holding her legs and gazing down at her feet. Presently she looked up at us.
'Is it a miracle?' she asked in an awed voice.

It wasn't long before Jeannie **ran from flowers to flowers; she skipped and sang and laughed for pure joy.**

One day Frances found her in a sober mood standing in her garden:

'I've come to see you, Sister.' There was a pause. Her eyes regarded me with direct candour. 'I've just realised something.'

I waited.

'I've realised that I'm not dreaming,' she said quietly. 'I'm dead.' Her gaze held mine. 'We're all dead. That's true, isn't it?'

'Yes. It's true, Jeannie,' I answered her, 'but you see we're really more alive than ever. You've only got rid of your sick old body and found a new one. ...'

She accepted this.

'I suppose this is ...a sort of Heaven.'

'It's the *beginning* of Heaven, Jeannie.'

'You mean we're only *starting*? ... We're not *there* yet?'

'Not in the Heaven you mean, Jeannie. But we're on our way there.'

She digested this. 'But it's so beautiful here. Everyone's so kind and ... and ... angelic.'

'We're certainly not angels,' I retorted and we both laughed at that. She was quiet suddenly.

'Then where's God?' she demanded.

'Much too far away for us even to see Him. We're not ready for His glory yet. But we're all going forwards, on towards His Heaven. ...'

But not directly, as we shall see in a moment. There are dance festivals in the astral world, and Jeannie is looking forward to them. She hopes to perfect her skills with hard work at the Halls of Beauty:

'Oh, it will be lovely! I'll work so hard and I'll be good. I do mean to be ready soon. Of course, I'll miss you and Sister Hilda and Mother Florence and everybody, but I want to go so much. I must go soon. You see,' she stopped dancing, quietened and stood still before me, 'You see, I've got to be perfect at dancing before ...' she broke off.
'Before what, dear?'
'Before I go back to earth again ... really to be a dancer.'
For a while I was silenced, overwhelmed by the wisdom of this child.

So there it is: reincarnation. The subject is treated in depth on the last page of the scripts:

So many units [souls] return again and again to the nothingness of dense matter [earth conditions], bravely asserting the lasting reality of their illumination. So often such units, clothed in their passing personalities, fall into ignorance, becoming subject to materialistic concepts. Some are blessed on their journeys by flashes into the Light, and in rare cases, the Light gained in these spiritual Worlds holds steady, shining through the fleshly masks to bless and encourage their fellow travelers in the darkness . ... Light shines from the eyes of these advanced egos, and is reflected in the magnetic fields which surround their dense bodies.

On another occasion Frances tells of meeting old friends and former teachers from former lives, but she also makes it clear that not everyone in her world must reincarnate. For some there is **swift progress to other and higher spheres.** Frances herself is determined to be among that number, and six months after her death it's clear she's made progress in that direction. She tells us she is growing out of her old astral body into something more real:

I realise that what is passing from me, like sloughing a skin, is insubstantial, impermanent, decomposing, as it drops from me into a dusty nothingness. What is left is essentially Light, is Reality, is permanent and is true. I call this my new Body of Light and that, indeed, is what it truly is. A Body of Light, not dense and material and dull and heavy as the physical body, not insubstantial, shadowy and unreal as the astral body in which I have been sheltering, but brilliant, 'encelled' with Light, ethereal in that there is no weight, no dragging down into matter but is enmeshed with colour and beauty into form and substance. Is that a difficult conception? You must remember that I am forming this, my spiritual Body, or should I be more correct in saying I am merging into it.

It doesn't sound as if Frances will veer back toward earth anytime soon!

Nevertheless, reincarnation, Frances tells us, is a living option in her world. What does that say about Christian doctrine, which assumes only a single earth life? Frances has much to say about the dogmas of earth's religions:

There are no tenets, no creeds, no formulae, no hard and fast rules devised by any mind to restrict or confine progress here. ... No soul is coerced, forced or bound by creeds. ... Helpers and Teachers and Great Souls there are in number to explain such errors of thinking, but there are no rules to follow and obey except the Divine Precept of Love, Light, Wisdom and Understanding.

So you don't have to believe that Jesus Christ is your Lord and Savior in order to be saved, or that there is no god but Allah and that Muhammad is his prophet to avoid damnation. In her world, beliefs don't mean anything by themselves. All that counts is the sort of life they coax or inspire out of you. Frances, incidentally, doesn't feel that she has ceased to be a Christian in the afterlife. Now she is free, as she puts it, **to find the far more glorious truths which are inherent in the Christian religion.**

But others, though just as free, will not be attracted to those truths. Frances tells us that many of these will have been people of prominence back on earth, and often their prominence will have been undeserved. But in this new world deception is impossible. Your aura broadcasts to all you meet exactly what kind of being you are. This is one of the most interesting, and frightening, features of Frances's world: the impossibility of posturing. Everyone's character sticks out like the proverbial sore thumb. She puts it this way: **In the earth life he can build a façade about himself. Here he has no such mask. He is known here for what he is, and for what *his inner subjective* life has made him.** We see into each other as we imagined only God could. The best preparation for such a world, the best way to avoid the embarrassment of being found out, is, she tells us, **the inner life of meditation and contemplation and at-one-ment with Divine Beauty and Truth.** A tall order! One that helps us understand why so many souls find themselves more comfortable in the Shadowlands! It's not surprising that many prefer the anonymity of the dark astral regions to the all-revealing Light of the higher spheres.

In an earlier chapter the deceased Frederic Myers introduced us to the notion of a Group Soul: an extended family of souls – sometimes ranging into the thousands – living in intimacy with each other and trustingly sharing their experiences. Frances confirms what Myers says. Her description of the move from the cottage with its garden where she spent her first months to her Group is especially interesting:

> ... whilst I was meditating in my golden garden, I found myself 'transported' to ... a cluster of entities about a

Teacher. Immediately I experienced a rise of consciousness, an upsurge of joy, a mingling of unity and harmony which coloured my whole being. I cannot explain this in any other terms, though I doubt whether they will have the same connotation for you. I knew this was right for me. I had come into my own. There was no definite acceptance, the entire operation was unobtrusive and simple, yet I had the conviction that all was well, that I was amidst my fellow-travellers on the Way.

Members of the Group **share a beautiful estate with ... wide sloping grass lands, trees and flowers of the most exquisite beauty and avenues of Light.** As for occupations, she finds herself **at the Halls of Learning almost continually.** She often travels:

I have visited countries of the world which I did not know. I have seen much and learned much. I return often to familiar scenes. I attend some Meetings and Meditation Groups and sometimes ... endeavour to reach the minds of old and dear friends still in physical existence. Sometimes I am happy to think that my efforts meet with a certain response. At others the veil of illusion interferes and the contact is faulty, or is even rejected.

This passage is a good segue into another of Frances's favorite teachings. Not only can we earthlings be helped by little nudges, invitations, and inspirations sent telepathically from the world of spirits; our prayers for the 'dead' can also have a therapeutic effect on them, especially on those who **dwell in darkness.** Unfortunate are those spirits who have no one remembering or praying for them, Frances tells us.

Perhaps you've noticed that the word *Light* is always capitalized. Since the title of Frances's book is *Testimony of Light*, it's fitting to conclude this chapter with a few words about the Light's nature.

Remember that Frances told little Jeannie that their world is far removed from God's. One gets the impression that, as nice as their world is, it's just a humble anteroom to the True Heaven where something as sublime as God dwells. There is a becoming modesty throughout this book. Clearly Frances has a long, long way to go before she reaches her goal, and she knows it. Her world is a kind of beatific purgatory.

Nevertheless, her world is much closer to God than ours is. We don't think of sunlight as divine, but the spiritual Light of Frances's world is. It's this Light that Frances thinks of herself as evolving toward. This Light is God's ambience. We hardly see it at all because earth's slower vibrations shut it out and leave us in a densely material environment, but Frances, living in an astral environment where light vibrates faster, can. She tells us: **I feel as though I am starting on a Path of Light which leads upwards and onwards into Realms of unimaginable beauty and wonder and of which I have, as yet, but the faintest glimmer of comprehension. The journey itself is compensation enough for the trials of earth.**

Here she makes it clear that the Path of Light she is traveling on – she means her world as opposed to ours – is nothing compared to the infinitely glorious, utterly indescribable Light that is to come. This last Light is no reflection, no ambience. Rather it is what Frances calls **the eternal Centre of Light and Creative Energy which men call God.** It is the full blast of the Godhead Itself. As she tells it, **we progress onwards and upwards into that Divine Self, after aeons of endeavour, into inclusion in the Divine Company, into bliss which is inexplicable at our present stage of understanding.**

But the Light of Frances's world is not distant, remote, or inaccessible to her *where she is* – as the quotations above might make it seem. On the contrary, it penetrates her; it is to be found within her. She describes it this way:

This is a wonderful, thrilling experience. When I caught but a glimpse of Light on earth, and it uplifted and changed me, and changed also the direction of my life, that impermanent glimpse was as *nothing* to the *immersion* of Light that is possible here. I appear to lie in my garden, yet in the power of this Light, my mind and spirit stretch out into a glorious extension.

The Light she describes here is no mere impersonal energy either. Though transpersonal, it has a definite motherly quality about it. It comforts her. **I rest in that Light and am healed from my many mistakes,** she tells us.

This is a mind-blowing book. It is full of surprises, full of descriptions that the human imagination would be very hard pressed to dream up. For example, Frances tells us that the Light of her world is not only visible; you can hear it. She tells us that during festivals of music, one doesn't just sing as we do: **One is singing with the whole organism.** Whatever that means! Occasionally she overreaches herself and just stammers.

I use this book as the capstone of my university course The Meaning of Death. I have never been tempted to change it.

Chapter 7

What the Protestant Theologian Discovered upon Dying

I've read many books on this subject. This is one of the best, both because of its compelling believability and the practical advice given to help us prepare for the journey. This is a stimulating book with a great message for everyone.
Elda Hartley

The primary communicator here was the notable Lutheran minister, theologian, and professor Alvin D. (AD) Mattson, who died in October 1970. An author in this life, he became one in the next as well. His postings from the Other Side were collected by his daughter, Ruth Mattson Taylor, and published in two books – the first, *Witness from Beyond*, in 1975. We'll be working mainly out of that book, though the second, *Evidence from Beyond*, published 24 years later, provides an important corrective to the earlier work. The medium through whom AD spoke was Margaret Flavell, a devout Methodist and graduate of the London School of Paranormal Psychology and Sanctuary of Healing. A born clairvoyant, she was commissioned during World War II to trace missing Air Force pilots, and was often successful. She was a rare 'positive medium,' meaning she was fully conscious when spirits spoke through her: She had the ability to block out her own thoughts while the spirit communicator used her mind. She died only recently, at the age of 94. Both Mattson and Flavell were persons of the highest integrity. Neither had ever met each other.

In life AD developed an interest in psychic phenomena while

a graduate student at Yale, and he was convinced enough that we all survive death to promise that 'when he died he was surely going to try to communicate back to earth.' Would he follow through with his promise? Taylor and Flavell would give him the chance. In Taylor's words,

> Not quite five months after AD died, Margaret Flavell, a close friend from London, was visiting us. She is one of the most respected clairvoyants in England and has a remarkable record of accomplishments in the field of psychic communication. We had expected to make contact with him and to get evidence that he does survive, but little did we expect the quantity and quality of very significant communication and information that we received. From March 1971 through October 1973 we received fifty-five communications amounting to over five hundred legal-sized pages of typed manuscripts. For this book we have extracted the material we felt would be of interest to the general reader. Communications of a very personal nature, relating to our immediate family, have been deleted.

On one occasion Hartley Productions filmed Flavell channeling AD, with Taylor recording on tape the message. Sitting straight-backed in a chair, Flavell speaks without a break, as if reading a well-prepared sermon. *Witness from Beyond* needed very little copy editing.

The messages from AD were full of evidential material, leaving no doubt in Taylor's mind that this was indeed her father. The best of it is examined in an appendix.

One of the most appealing features of the book – one that sets it apart from those early, more abstract revelations like *Spirit Teachings* – is the descriptions of astral geography. On rare occasions someone other than AD comes through, and on the second sitting his wife, Taylor's mother, spoke. She tried to convey the beauty of her world:

> **AD has gone off to 'refresh' himself. I don't know what he calls refreshment, but I'll tell you what my refreshment is. It is walking around our lake and watching the fish jump. We have a beautiful lake here. It is a lovely blue sky color. At the moment the weeping willows are out and down-hanging, and the flowers are so beautiful.**

A little later during the same sitting, Flavell received a direct impression, a picture, of this spirit woman taking her walk:

> **She is very slender. Not thin, but slender. I still see the back of her. She looks quite small as if I'm away in the distance looking at her. She is at the far end of the lake now, and she's looking at the spring coming in. There is a little bridge there, rather like a Chinese bridge over the water. It's made of wood and it's lacquered. It's a beautiful green and yellow. The whole place appears to be shimmering.**

Much of what this books describes we've seen before, as we would expect if the world to come is real and not a subjective hallucination, varying radically from person to person. For example, AD views his own funeral, as did Frances Banks. Dear friends and family await his 'homecoming.' The distinction between the Third and Fourth spheres so vividly traced by Frederic Myers is easily recognized here, even though the terminology is different. Hellish domains or 'Shadowlands,' which have turned up in almost all our readings, turn up here too. Libraries, pets, great architecture, other planets, earthbound spirits, various levels of vibration, astral clothing, spirit guides and guardians, and many other themes we've found in earlier chapters are found here too. Typical afterlife occupations mentioned by AD include **nurses, botanists, librarians,**

ministers, musicians, and artists. But all is not work in the spiritual world. **There are periods for relaxation and play there, too, and particularly for the young people, who enjoy many of the activities they knew on earth.**

The astral world is almost a replica of your world, AD tells us, **except that it is of a finer substance and we are not 'bound' by our objective reality here.** Churchman that he was, it is perhaps not surprising to hear that **we have denominations on this plane and we continue to practice the rites of our respective churches.** There are even **great cathedrals and great churches** where ministers **who preached on earth, and still feel the urge to do so, continue to preach.** And our body is also familiar: **The astral body in which we live immediately after we have died is a duplicate of our physical body, except that it is made of a fine, tenuous substance.**

To further questions about this body, he explains: **We don't think of putting food into our mouths, because it isn't needed. Therefore, the whole of the astral digestive tract and the elimination organs, like the kidneys and colon, cease to function. ... However, we continue to use the psychic centers of the body. These become much more active because they are now free of the physical body.**

A central concern in this book is what you would expect of a devout Christian clergyman. From the beginning AD is eager to help and heal. He says, **We are just as much morally obligated to help our brothers on earth when we are without a physical body as we were within a physical body.** He gives two examples of such help, the first from the afterlife of his own father, also a minister in earth life, and long since deceased. AD tells us his father is focusing on the survivors of the great tidal wave that swallowed up 300,000 Bangladeshis during a cyclone in 1971. This example reveals how spirits can, and do, help us in practical ways all the time, even though we never guess it: **He gets in touch with them and gives them little impressions to make** them realize that the sun is high and it's time they got things done. He is not dealing with them when they're dead. He is dealing with those who are still living [on earth]. He has a fine group of associates with him who work to help them in their sleep. The second example is taken from the life of a cousin of his, Bill Hoag. Bill, who did in 1942, feels called upon to help those crippled by war: Bill helps those war casualties [from the Vietnamese War?] who still have to stay on earth and are not allowed to come over to us yet. This is a very tedious and very special kind of work. These wounded people have to be given the courage and strength to go on living, even though they may be badly crippled. AD himself can't make up his mind how to help when he first comes over: I find the latitude in our choices here to be quite incredible. I don't know what field I will enter at the present time. I will have to pray over this and inquire into various fields, because once we are committed, we are committed for a considerable time. Here we don't work so much as individuals. We work more in bands and groups. Eventually he decides to work with a group analyzing hunger problems and tries to transfer, telepathically, their solutions to specialists on earth working on the same problem from their end. The silent transfer to earth of helpful ideas is a common activity of spirits, as we've seen in previous chapters.

This transfer of wholesome thinking is acutely important in dealing with drug addicts and alcoholics, on both sides of the veil. The addicted don't lose their cravings just because they drop their dense earth bodies; their astral bodies are just as hooked. Such souls

stay near the earth to be near alcoholics or drug addicts who are still in the physical body, in order to participate vicariously in the sensations which alcohol and drugs give. They can be helped in the world beyond to clear their astral bodies of these cravings so they, too, may go on and progress. However, this is a long and tedious process.

AD's concerns go well beyond the addicted, however. He sees large groups of spirits who have no notion that the spirit world has joys of its own, with endless opportunities for spiritual, artistic, ethical, and intellectual growth. Many of these come from cultures that provided no opportunity for such growth while on earth. This is what AD says about them:

Many people from backward and underprivileged areas of the world find themselves unable to adapt to life after death when they first pass over. Due to environmental circumstances on earth, they have not had the opportunity to grow and develop, and have often 'vegetated' on earth. The dull, routine type of existence they have had puts them in a frame of mind to stay earthbound after death, near old familiar surroundings where they find a sense of comfort. However, this holds them back from any progress they could make in the spiritual world. We have many working here to try to help these people. When you are praying, send out a thought that power may go to all those who are working to release these backward, earthbound spirits so that they, too, can move forward and on.

But it's not just the underprivileged from the 'Third World' who need help. Ever the counselor, AD is just as concerned for privileged souls who made mistakes that now haunt them. He especially addresses the **sins of dogmatism ... procrastination ... [and] omission.** He tells us we undergo **a sort of self-judgment** shortly after we die, and that it's essential to forgive ourselves, since nothing good can come from hanging on to guilt. He strongly advises us to forgive each other before we die, since it's much harder after. What he says about sins of omission is instructive for us right here and now:

When any individual, on earth or here, omits doing something that he feels and knows he should do, the whole creation feels the loss. Whereas when we do something that adds grandeur and stature to life, the whole created universe gains from that action. It can make you shiver inside to know and appreciate how far-reaching a thought or deed or word of any person can be.

Another kind of temptation assails many of us throughout an average day and often leads to 'sins' of unkind thinking or wishing. Such sins, though scarcely noticed in our world, go around like big, heavy, sluggish pieces of material – like mud or oil slicks. Thoughts that radiate love, truth, compassion, and understanding leave a glow within us and around us and act like a force to remove the thought forms which are not constructive. AD describes an experience he had while flying over one particular city (not named):

> … it was like swimming through a sewer. … My guide suggested that I take a look and find where some of the darker places were, and to my surprise many were coming from small groups of houses, places of business, and some schools. In these places there were rebellion, disillusionment, and anger. From these areas rose visual colors that were gray and heavy, and anger produced a fiery red.

In contrast to such colors, where there was a feeling of love, the colors which rose were blue and violet. … Know that when you sit for meditation and for prayer, that goes out into the ether. It will be picked up by your next-door neighbor, others farther away, and also by those unseen ones passing overhead.

There is no indication in any of this that AD and his cohorts are working as specifically Christian missionaries, either for our benefit or for those on his side of the veil. His personal religion, however, is another thing; and it is interesting to see how it broadens over the two and a half years we hear from him. In an early communication he tells us, **I have seen the Lord Jesus in all his radiance, in all his glory.** He reports that the vision produced **an indescribable contentment and uplifting, a tremendous ecstasy of feeling ... an unusually vivid knowledge of the intense, sympathetic love around you.** Upon analyzing what happened to him, he adds,

> **He shows himself to us according to our own understanding. If I want to think of him as a man who walked by the lake and a man who looked as the Jews looked at that time, then I'll see him that way. If in my thought I think he's modern and bright, then I'll see him that way. ... To me he came walking across the air – across the tops of the buildings, the trees.**

In another early communication he says of Jesus,

> **You have heard some people say that they feel it doesn't make any difference whether Jesus was or was not. When they do this, they are placing themselves in a trap. They will say, 'I have faith in God and I don't need any intermediaries.' Fine. Perhaps they don't need any saints, but how can they cut out the light of the world – Jesus, the Christ? How *can* they?**

This narrow view of salvation gives way in later communications. Here we get a look at how AD's vision has broadened:

> **I am still utterly amazed at what I find here. Utterly amazed! There is love and there is harmony. There is music that transcends all thought. There is color, light, belonging, and there is being. It isn't only in the one path of Christianity.**

You find it in many, many other faiths. All faiths which stress love have this focus. It is like reaching out to a sun and light comes down along different rays.We are all walking. We Christians walk here, the Hindus walk there, the Buddhists walk in another place, and so forth. All have their own paradise, goals, aims, and objectives for so long. Then suddenly they are into the tremendous experience of knowing that all is one under God and that there is no division in purpose.

Since I have been out of the body, it has been my great fortune to have this communion – this attunement and 'at-one-ment' with souls and minds that have been treading a different way, having different beliefs and different concep-tions. It is a tremendous, knowing revelation and a great joy to have this understanding, warmth, and at-one-ment. There is one God of us all.

This example shows one of the many ways that souls grow in the afterlife. I have yet to come across in any of my research a spirit whose religious perspective *narrowed*. AD's growth is typical, even predictable.

In several of his communications AD described meeting fellow theologians and churchmen, one of them Martin Luther, the founder of Protestantism 500 years ago. (Remember that AD was a *Lutheran* minister and theologian in life.) He describes a convocation **of about 20,000 Lutherans who had gathered together** to hear Luther speak. During his life on earth Luther, though writing some of the most inspired religious tracts in religious history, denounced Catholics and Jews with vitriolic fervor. But that's not the Luther we meet here. AD tells us that Luther **expressed a desire for an expansion of consciousness, for barriers to be knocked down.** Now AD finds him to be a most tolerant mind and very understanding, but still fiery. He is far beyond what I had conceived from his writings. I find him still an electrifying force, a great awakener. He is a great soul. When I think of him, and when I think of the work he did, then it overwhelms me with my inadequacy and the inadequacy of all of us to translate the tremendous thoughts that he brought.

But it's not only the greats of the world that AD encounters in the afterlife. At the other end of the spectrum, he finds house pets:

> ... all the dogs that we've had in our family I can find here – all of them. They are still individualized. However, the dogs that I knew as a boy are no longer here. When I asked why, I was told that they have gone back to the group soul and have added their quota of affection, love, and devotion, to be used again when other dogs come to earth.

House pets retain their individuality as long as they are remembered and loved.

From animals to outer space – AD has something to say on almost every subject! After learning to **travel by swift thought – to wing the spirit – and ... arrive very quickly anywhere on the surface of the globe,** he formed the desire to go into outer space. This wish attracted a guide, and they were off:

> Suddenly – I don't know how it happened – the two of us were out into the deepest of indigo blue, and yet we could see. ... I could see the stars ... they seemed more alive and were vibrating out at me. ... Suddenly I was ... looking down. There below me was the moon, with a very slow-moving, milky kind of mistiness around it. ... I could also see the earth and it was blue.

At the height of this experience he felt intense exhilaration, and immediately he found himself alone and back where he started from, mission accomplished. But not before he remembered hearing an extraordinary symphony while out in space. Once again we are reminded of the special place that music holds in the afterlife, but not music quite like we've ever known it:

> There was a tremendous harmony of sound. It would be impossible to say that it was a symphony, or that it was a chorale, or that I could translate it into music that would go on a treble or a bass clef – that would be impossible. It was more like the most perfect sound that could come, not from a machine such as a huge organ but rather from a living, moving organism.

What AD is describing here we have no idea. Apparently the afterlife will hold many a surprise for us!

On one occasion AD traveled to other inhabited planets. He found that **there are inhabitants on many millions of planets, and some are very different from us on Earth.** All of them, he tells us, **are under the one creative force that we call God.** He continues:

> There are social bonds among the peoples we contacted, just as there are on Earth. There is also evidence of some moral struggle and evolvement among these inhabitants. We learned that we can, with permission, make a decision to incarnate on another planet in another galaxy, if we wish. Some do. However, each planet was populated by the Creator in its own unique way. A permanent change of form would be necessary to shift to living in another environment. We found that illness strikes other body forms, just as it does the human form. There were hospitals or healing centers wherever we found an inhabited planet,

so there is no 'perfect' body form that does not have a few problems now and then.

But AD has no desire to reincarnate on one of these distant planets. He says, **I'm glad I made the journey, but I feel that Earth and its atmosphere are my true home.**

At the outset of this chapter we mentioned that AD spoke to us in two books, the second, *Evidence from Beyond,* published 24 years after the first. Let's delve into the second for a moment to see what AD says about a subject that interests most of us, but that has so far been neglected.

In the first book there is no mention of reincarnation – no pronouncement for or against it. How surprising, then, to find whole chapters in the second given over to the concept. The editor, Ruth Taylor (AD's daughter), explains, 'We didn't include any of the earliest communications on reincarnation in *Witness from Beyond,* because A.D. wished it to be a handbook on the concept of survival after death and he didn't want material in it that might confuse his message.'

Here is AD's first reference to reincarnation:

I have had several interesting contacts here with my brother Karl, but his field of work is completely different. He is primarily concerned with assisting highly developed souls leaving earth. I think that eventually my own main interest is going to be not in helping those who have just left the earth, but in helping those who are going back down to earth. ... Right now, I'm in contact with those who are just beginning their descent at about the second or third month of pregnancy.

AD later shows an awareness of past incarnations. **I'm the sum total,** he tells us, **of my life and thoughts as A.D., plus some that I have gathered from other lives.**

But why do souls reincarnate? AD is clear on the point, and what he says is the classic answer we hear from other communicators:

> It's an interesting fact that most persons grow faster spiritually while incarnate. The incarnate energy is denser. That makes it more possible for you, while embodied in flesh on earth, to take hold of a particular problem area and shape it into a more constructive pattern. Your period of incarnation on the physical plane is thus a very important period of education. It contributes to your own spiritual evolution and that of all humanity. You can elect not to return, and many do, after they have achieved a certain spiritual development. But the physical plane is a 'school' for learning and development, and so most souls do desire to return for a series of incarnations.

Reincarnation is even the explanation for homosexuality:

> Some souls coming into incarnation as women still keep in the core of their being a desire for a close, loving, caring relationship with another woman. Their experiences in male/female relationships in other lives may have been hurtful and debasing … they reach back to imprints of a past incarnation where they experienced happiness with an all-female group. … Likewise, some men, because of imprints of past incarnations and the customs of those times, come into incarnation and seek comfort, sustenance, and peace with another like-minded male. … Often, the spiritual evolution of persons with this orientation can't progress unless the feeling of drawing together man with man and woman with woman is fulfilled.

As in every other communicator examined in this book, the purpose of our lives, whether in one or many incarnations, is to grow the soul. AD puts it this way:

> ... the essence of all is like a thread, and we may see ourselves as beautiful beads on that thread or we can see ourselves as very heavy pieces of lead, noncomprehending, depending on the degree to which we are in tune with the universe and the laws God has lain down ... the ultimate goal in the evolution of man is to reach the point where each man, each sacred personality created, is in tune and is, as it were, a beautiful bead on the thread of the essence of the whole.

The two books in which AD shines through have been favorites among discerning readers of after-death communications. His writing is vivid and fascinating, his interests are consistent with his life's work on earth, and his descriptions of the afterlife jibe with those of others we've read where you would expect them to.

Conclusion

... the stream of knowledge is heading towards a non-mechanical reality; the Universe begins to look more like a great thought than like a great machine. Mind no longer appears to be an accidental intruder into the realm of matter ... we ought rather hail it as the creator and governor of the realm of matter.
Sir James Jeans

Let's summarize what we have learned from our seven spirit sources about life after death. The following points are not exhaustive, but they strike me as the most important – and interesting – of the bunch.

1. The Afterworld is not some fantastic vision of infinity where souls are locked in poses of permanent rapture gazing at the face of God. And no one floats on a cloud while playing a harp. Rather it is a place with landscapes and seas and houses and cities reminiscent of our own world – a material world, but of higher vibration insensible to us earthlings. There are gardens, universities, libraries, and hospices for the newly dead – but no factories, fire stations, sanitary landfills, or smokestacks. There are no dirty jobs to do. **We have no traffic, and our roads are covered with the thickest and greenest grass, as soft to the feet as a bed of fresh moss. It is on these that we walk,** says Msgr. Hugh Benson, as we saw earlier. All accounts describe a world of exquisite natural beauty.

2. The Afterworld begins at the earth's surface and extends outward. Earth is the nucleus of the entire world system that the spirits describe.

3. Spirits do not usually refer to their world as heaven. Their world is actually a spectrum of realms stretching from the lowly joys and satisfactions of a novice soul just come over; to spheres of unimaginable radiance, perfection, and fulfillment that they

have only heard about or at best visited; to darker, murkier regions where souls of a lower order reside.

4. Earth's slow vibrations dumb down our ability to sense the presence of spirit, including the Divine. A quickened vibration, such as we find in the Afterworld, or what we shall call the astral, greatly increases one's sensitivity to spirit. The Divine is no closer to the astral world than to our own, but spirits can discern or intuit It more cleanly.

5. The newly 'dead' are thoroughly themselves when they pass. Their personalities and habits and character, for better or worse, are completely intact. Nothing miraculous happens to them when they pass. Their astral body is not a 'resurrected' body, but was always present as the soul's 'inner envelope' while embodied in earthly flesh. Once the physical body dies, the inner body quite naturally becomes the outer – as a snake's inner skin becomes the outer skin once it sheds the old.

6. Spirits are not omniscient. They don't get the answers to all the questions that puzzled them back on earth just because they've died. Many fail to grasp their condition; some, especially those who were certain that death meant extinction, even refuse to believe they have died. For, as we have seen, the landscapes of the astral world are similar to the landscapes of earth they left behind.

7. Though they are recognizably themselves, life in the astral is more vivid and intense than on earth, not more ghostly. Astral beings have fewer limitations. They can communicate telepathically and with much greater precision than through the cumbersome medium of speech. They can move from place to place by willing to be at their destination, though they can walk if they want to. Their minds are sharper, their emotions more acutely felt, both positive and negative. They see and hear as before, but in a more intense way.

8. The old or decrepit or injured bodies they left behind do not follow them beyond death. Yet they *are* embodied, almost always

in a manner that makes them recognizable by others who knew them on earth. At all times they bear with them an astral signature that identifies who they are.

9. The Creator places souls in the difficult environment of earth because He (She, It) loves them. He wants to see them grow in wisdom, love, and power. He knows that the only way to bring out the best in a soul is to challenge it, in the same way that a good teacher challenges her students. Ultimately the Creator wants us to become as much like Himself/Herself as possible, to grow into near divine-like stature. Soul-building, or character development, is the whole point of our sojourn, both on earth and beyond. The use we make of our free will is absolutely crucial to our progress at all levels.

10. AD Mattson's trip to other inhabited planets revealed a divine plan very much like the one just sketched. I am less than confident that Mattson in reality took such a trip, but if he did – if the 'trip' wasn't the product of mediumistic contamination, as discussed in the Introduction – then what he found is what I would expect him to find. For the divine plan, I should think, would be consistent throughout the universe.

11. The Afterworld is a broad-based society of every conceivable kind of person, most of them flawed and incomplete in some way or another. Many are no more motivated to 'grow their souls' than they were back on earth. But the best are determined to advance.

12. Spirits are not allowed to overreach in the astral, but must grow in wisdom and in love gradually. They cannot enter a vibration or cross a boundary they are not ready for. There is justice in where they end up at death. There is definitely a law of karma. They gravitate to their rightful place. They can move ahead only when they are changed enough to do so.

13. Many of them had ambitious plans for self-improvement before they descended into flesh, but the density of earth's matter, including their own dense brain, caused them to forget

what they came for. Subject to material concepts, they lost their way. They died only to discover to their disappointment that they mostly failed to accomplish the goal they had set for themselves. But for many of them it's OK, for there has been much growth in unpremeditated ways.

14. The astral world provides opportunities for every wholesome interest or avocation – from science to music to theology to astral architecture to homebuilding. It is a joyful, endlessly fascinating place, full of challenges, for those who desire to grow.

15. Physical danger does not exist in the astral. Neither does physical illness. Eating is optional and sleep unnecessary. The calls of nature do not get even a mention.

16. Many astral inhabitants maintain a lively interest in the events of earth and long to help it progress. They claim that many or even most of earth's most brilliant achievements were inspired by spirits telepathically projecting their ideas. Nor do 'the dead' forget their loved ones, whom they often seek to help with what we might call prayer in reverse.

17. Spirits do not meet an embodied personal God in the astral world. Instead many find themselves surrounded by an all-pervasive, penetrating Divine Light, full of understanding and love. This Light does not judge them, at least from the outside. They seem to judge themselves. As spirits advance, they move ever closer to the heart of the Creator.

18. They celebrate the presence of that Light in powerful rituals involving supremely grand music and displays of light, described in astonishing language. Music seems to be the supreme art of the astral, with most communicators noting its inspirational quality. According to Benson sound and light are coextensive: the astral is synesthetic. Painting, dance, theater, and architecture are also prominently mentioned. It is safe to say that the more refined a person's aesthetic taste is in this life, the more at home he or she will feel in the higher realms of the astral.

19. Benson speaks at length about theater in the astral, especially historical productions. Special delight is afforded by theater that places history as earth understands it next to history as it really happened. The latter is available only in the astral.

20. A premium is placed on reading. The acquisition of knowledge, insight, and wisdom must be worked at in the astral; it must be earned. On the other hand, as we've seen, the astral mind is far sharper than the earthly one, and learning comes quickly, leaves a vivid impression, and is not forgotten.

21. There are hellish regions in the astral, and large populations that make their home there. What is sometimes referred to as the Shadowlands is a vast world of many conditions. The landscapes vary from sordid city neighborhoods to parched, gray scrubland to dark, lifeless deserts. The vivid clarity of higher realms is missing. Instead there is a dull overcast. Temporarily lost or confused or stubbornly unrepentant souls populate these regions.

22. Some of these souls aggressively seek to harm vulnerable humans on earth. They band together to **resist progress and truth, and fight against the dissemination of what advantages humanity,** as Imperator puts it in Chapter 1.

23. Missionary spirits minister to souls in the Shadowlands. Residents can free themselves if they are willing to face up humbly to their errors and crimes and repent them. Some do; and most, perhaps all, will eventually. But many jeer at their would-be helpers and seem to prefer their dull lives over the challenges of higher worlds they are frightened of.

24. One form of experience in the lower astral is a descent into gross pleasure devoid of spiritual content. Myers describes a man who was obsessed with sex on earth, sex with anybody. Astral sex to the point of stupefying satiety is a real possibility. What starts out as pleasurable ends up being disgusting and revolting.

25. Some spirits tell us that no spirit remains forever in the dark regions. But God will never interfere with our free will.

S/He will invite tirelessly, but will never force.

26. There are three basic ways to progress in the Afterworld: admitting defects in one's character, service to others, and yearning for higher states. Service to others demands effort, work, sacrifice. Nowhere do the spirits describe a deity who requires us to flatter or glorify him with our prayers. That is not the way to progress.

27. There are no rigid creeds or magical beliefs that souls have to accept. Whether you are a Baptist or a Catholic or a Mormon or a Hindu or a Buddhist or a Muslim or an Anglican is of no importance. Many of earth's favorite religious dogmas are off the mark anyway, and the sooner they are recognized as such, the better. Experience in the Afterworld will generate, as a matter of course, a more enlightened set of beliefs that will better reflect the way things really are than any of earth's theologies.

28. There are no masks in the astral. You cannot hide from others what you are: the quality of light shining forth from your body tells all. Even the house a spirit lives in reflects his spiritual stature. These facts can be humiliating at first, but it spurs spirits on to a greater effort to improve themselves.

29. The sense of earth time fades fast. There is duration, but nothing like clock-time with its schedules and deadlines.

30. Spouses, relatives, friends, and former teachers, some from earlier lives, some long forgotten, turn up and may renew old friendships. If two persons linked by love to each other on earth want to continue the relationship after death and are, roughly speaking, spiritual equals, there is nothing stopping them.

31. Many spirits are members of large spirit families, or **Group Souls,** that await them when they pass. They feel as if they have come home when they are received by the familiar group.

32. Spirits in the astral meet Christ-like beings, Beings of Light far advanced, teachers who come down from higher

worlds to inspire progress toward realms of incomparably greater joy and awareness.

33. As they progress in the next world, they eventually slough off their astral body, just as they sloughed off their physical body at physical death. Then they will operate out of a spiritual body of lesser density with a greater capacity for joy and awareness.

34. Spirits are not naked, but clothed. Astral clothing is fashioned by the mind. There are no clothes closets in the astral.

35. Our prayers for those who have passed are efficacious and deeply appreciated. If forgotten by their earth friends and family, spirits can experience loneliness.

36. Children of all ages are raised in the Afterworld. They are not magically transformed into adults just because they died prematurely. One of the noblest professions in the astral is nurturing and educating spirit orphans. Great numbers of spirits are engaged in this satisfying form of work.

37. The astral world is not a somber realm lacking laughter and merriment. As an example, astral theater pokes good-natured fun at earthly anxieties, which spirits now find hilarious. Entertainment also comes in diviner modes. Judge Hatch's Beautiful Being's **playthings** were **days and ages.** As for the spirits of young children, they delight in stories of that myste-rious planet earth, which almost became their home. **Nothing gives us more fun than when a party of young folk get together and relate their earth experiences,** says Leslie Stringfellow.

38. Many spirits continue to observe the **man-made forms of religion** they practiced on earth until they discover a deeper, fuller spirituality **purged of every trace of meaningless creed, of doctrines and dogmas,** says Msgr. Benson.

39. Yet Christians in the Afterworld continue to celebrate Christmas and Easter, though many reinterpret their meaning in a way that corresponds with their new understanding of Christ – not as God, but, according to Judge Hatch, as **a type of the greatest Master ... revered in all the heavens.** Some say they

have seen Jesus. Mattson saw him **walking across the air.** Mattson tells us that each of us will see Jesus as we think of him. Presumably that would hold true of other religious savior figures.

40. When a person commits suicide, he sends forth **his spirit alone and friendless into a strange world where no place was yet prepared for it ... in the end he fell prey to tempters in the spirit, who fastened on him and drove him to his ruin,** according to Imperator. There are warnings against suicide in most channeled literature. Yet there is hope for such a person, especially with the help of earth's prayers. Suicides do not end up in an eternal hell. But they do not resolve their problems either.

41. Human dilemmas turn up in the astral just as they do on earth. Judge Hatch described a man whose company was desired by both his former wives. Hatch was constantly being called on to help fellow spirits out of their emotional predicaments. His skills as an arbiter, learned on earth, served him well on the Other Side. You might also recall the Jewish mother riveted by hatred to her Nazi persecutor. It was the task of Frances Banks to pry her loose and teach her to forgive the man. Problem-solving is as necessary in the astral as on earth.

42. Spirits enjoy hobbies, knitting being one of them. There is plenty of time in the astral; boredom and even homesickness for earth are mentioned in these accounts.

43. The ultimate future of some spirits is stupendous beyond imagination. It's worth repeating what Myers said above: **you still exist as an individual [and] are wholly aware of the imagination of God. So you are aware of the whole history of the earth from Alpha to Omega. Equally all planetary existence is yours. Everything created is contained within that imagination, and you ... know it and hold it.**

44. What about reincarnation? As we are about to see, the subject will require special handling.

One of our seven sources (Benson/Borgia) says nothing about it and even implies that it doesn't occur. The other six do mention it, and five of those six endorse it. For those five, reincarnation is one of the keys to soul growth and is therefore crucial to the divine plan. If they are correct, how can Msgr. Benson, or any spirit for that matter, be 'out of the loop' on so fundamental a question? Or is his medium, Anthony Borgia, infecting Benson's message with an anti-reincarnation bias? If so, isn't it odd that Benson would continue to use him? But it could be the other way round. Perhaps the mediums used by the *other* spirits we've been looking at have a *pro*-reincarnation bias that leaks into their messages from the Other Side.

It is noteworthy that among Spiritualists the question of reincarnation has been a hot potato from the start, with many for it and many opposed. Spiritualists are just the experts we would expect unanimity from if the world of spirit runs according to some universal law that they have discovered. But that is not the case.

That is why a book like this one is necessary. We see our seven sources agreeing on most subjects, and that is critical for developing an idea of what follows death. But reincarnation is an exception. Why?

One possibility is that spirits speak to us from realms that differ from each other more than we might expect. Is it common for spirits residing in a Hindu realm to reincarnate, while just as common for spirits living in a Protestant Christian realm not to? Presumably the latter realm would be composed of Christians who never believed in reincarnation while on earth and do not think of it as an attractive or available option now that they have left earth. Msgr. Benson hints at something like this: **Thus far I have given you a few facts of my own knowledge derived from my own experience, and therefore what I have told you applies to the specific realm wherein I live.** Benson does not deny reincarnation; in fact he never mentions the word. He says only that as far as he is concerned death is **the casting off of the physical body, and entering, for all time, the world of spirit.** For him it might be. It might also be the case that at a future date he would change his mind and desire rebirth. Spirits do not claim to be able to see far into the future. Why should Benson know more about his personal future than we do ours? We cannot know what we will do in the distant future, and he cannot either.

What is completely clear is that our other spirit sources believe in it and have seen instances of it. Four of the seven are certain it is in their personal future. It is of course possible that all this apparent certainty derives from the biases of the mediums.

The research of Ian Stevenson is important for me. Stevenson, the University of Virginia parapsychologist who made a career out of investigating little children with memories of what felt to them like past lives, makes a strong case for reincarnation on purely scientific grounds. Anyone who reads his books will be hard pressed to explain how his children, thousands of them from all over the world, could be in possession of so much specific information that fits the facts pertaining to the alleged former life. Stevenson aside, channeled literature published over the last half century usually affirms reincarnation. Our Chapters 6 and 7 are typical of this trend.

For me, AD Mattson sums up my belief best: **You can elect not to return, and many do, after they have achieved a certain spiritual development. But the physical plane is a 'school' for learning and development, and so most souls do desire to return for a series of incarnations.** But they know going into flesh that rebirth will be no party. They desire to return to earth conditions not because it's going to be easy or fun, but because the challenge of earth's obstacles and limitations will bring, they hope, the best out of them. For a relatively mature soul, a return to earth might resemble the experience of a teacher starting a new term after summer vacation.

I wish I could report that there was unanimity on this very important subject, but the facts don't permit it. This lack is the main reason I leave open the possibility, however slight, that this entire literature could be coming from the subconscious beliefs of mediums rather than from spirits. There are many reasons for thinking otherwise, and they impress me far more than this lone thorn among so many flowers growing together harmoniously, but there is no denying the prick.

Sometimes I wonder if we are supposed to know what to expect after we die. Maybe it's part of the divine plan that we do not. Are the spirits who tell us about their world through mediums flouting the plan? Are they making it too easy on us? And isn't earth supposed to be that place where nothing comes easy? Not even the truth about ourselves? About our destiny?

Spirits do not agree with this assessment. On the contrary, they feel that life on earth in the best of circumstances is difficult enough. Adding more to the ordeal than is necessary is likely to retard our progress rather than advance it. Remaining ignorant of the divine plan is just such an unwelcome addition. Ignorance of the plan leaves us in the dark about why we struggle, why we suffer, why we fail, and why we die. Without insight into these mysteries, we are setting ourselves up for despair and character disintegration. The spirits know this, and that is why they try so hard to come through. For them it is natural that we should know in a general way what lies beyond death; it is in the Creator's plan that we should. The fact that so few of us do is a breach of the divine will, not its fulfillment.

Sometimes a skeptic will say that if we knew what to expect in the afterlife as a reward for virtue in this life, we would do the right thing for the wrong reason – for a selfish reason. That's not the way it feels to me. If I do the right thing, I do it because it is right. Believing that there is some sort of karmic reward for doing it only makes it easier to do. It doesn't determine me to do it; it merely adds incentive to do it. Mother Teresa's greatness was not diminished because she knew she was pleasing her God and preparing for herself a place in his heaven; there were hundreds of nuns in her order who shared that belief. What made her different wasn't some selfish calculation, but the clarity of her vision and the generosity of her heart. She did what she did because she saw with perfect clarity that it was the right thing to do. Her reward in heaven would be a nice side-effect, of course, but it was not the determinant of her heroic resolve.

I see no reason to keep secret the revelations that reach us from the spirit world. More than any religion I've studied or professed, they show me why we are on a planet like earth and what we must do here if we are to succeed.

Dag Hammarskjold, the second secretary-general of the United Nations and a man of great holiness, wrote, 'Only he who keeps his eye fixed on the far horizon will find the right road.' The 'far horizon' is the world of spirit, and what awaits us beyond that horizon depends on what kind of road we take. I believe the spirits we've looked at here show us that road.

A final question that many readers will be entertaining is the relation of Christian afterlife doctrine to what we've been reading here. If the spirits are correct, does it make sense to expect heaven or hell to commence at death, as most Protestant Christians have been taught? And are these domains rightly viewed as static worlds where there is no progress for either the damned or the saved? When I pose this question to my students, many say they aren't interested in further progress. For them heaven is an eternal resting place, and that is all they want. Progress? That sounds like work, and they're done with work! Others answer differently. They say that such an end would become unbearably boring after a spell, even if it was heavenly. On the whole, however, the popular version of the Christian's heaven is a place where the soul comes into possession of a joy in the presence of God that cannot be added to because it is already perfectly complete.

There is nothing in the literature we've been surveying here that supports this view of afterlife. At every level, it says, movement is expected. The will is just as free after death as before, and there are endless opportunities for further soul growth. Protestants, with their all-or-nothing, up-or-down view of the matter, have it all wrong.

What about Catholics and their purgatory? How does it match up against the message of the spirits? Is the afterlife experience better approximated by purgatory than heaven or hell? Purgatory is, after all, a process, not a final end. It is a place, a world, where spirits purge themselves of bad habits and tendencies and repent their mistakes. Of course, as most older Catholics will remember, purgatory was served up by their teachers as a kind of hell-with-an-ending – not just any process, but a very painful and long one classically described by Dante in lurid, appalling detail. Certainly that kind of purgatory doesn't fit what the spirits are trying to tell us here.

So none of these classical versions of the state of the soul after death is especially helpful. They rightly point to some kind of divine justice, but they are childlike in their simplicity and crude, even barbaric, in their execution. They are certainly not worthy of an all-wise, all-loving God who desires nothing so much as that we should freely turn toward the good, the beautiful, and the true as we work to uncover our native splendor so long imprisoned in one body after another, whether fleshly or astral or subtle. The spirits tell us, especially Imperator in Chapter 1 and Myers in Chapter 4, that we have the potential to become powerful, compassionate, joyous spirits as distant from what we are now as the butterfly from its larva. But the process of such evolution stretches over great expanses of time and requires steady effort. No soul is required to make this trek, but those who yearn to experience the divine life to the fullest degree possible for a creature will, like a great athlete, take the most challenging road to its objective. Is there ever a climax to the process? Does there come a point when the spirit merges its individuality with God's, whatever that might exactly mean, and finally rests? Does it really exist for all eternity as an individual? Myers wonders about that very thing, but he cannot say. All that comes across is the growing immensity and grandeur of the human soul when it responds continually to the call from its infinitely mighty and gracious Maker.

Imagine what our world would be like if young men and women were given the vision summarized here. Abraham Lincoln worked relentlessly to show young America that democracy at its best far surpassed any other form of government that the world had seen. His aim was to disseminate human happiness among the masses – former slaves, immigrants, Catholics, Jews. The spirits we've surveyed are inspired by something similar. They have a vision for bettering our world, for lifting the great mass of drifting, purposeless humanity toward a goal worthy of their native splendor. I hope they succeed.

Afterword

It is since Christians have largely ceased to think of the other world that they have become so ineffective in this.
C. S. Lewis

A few years ago Karen Armstrong, the celebrated religion writer, said that the question of an afterlife is 'a red herring' – something that distracts attention from important questions. An ex-Catholic nun severely critical of convent life, she went on to say she preferred 'to be agnostic' about an afterlife.

She continued: 'The religions say you can experience eternity in this life, here and now, by getting those moments of ecstasy when time ceases to be a constraint. And you do it by the exercise of the Golden Rule and by compassion. And just endless specu-lation about the next world is depriving you of a great experience in this one.'

What do we say to Armstrong?

First, she has a point. Zen is good at reminding us that all we have, after all, is the present moment. But the present moment does not exclude thinking about the future. Some of the most intense, important, creative moments in anyone's life are moments in which plans for the future are being hatched.

Second, she is correct in saying that people who get caught up in speculating about what an afterlife involves might be obsessing about it in an unhealthy way. But how many people actually do that? Is she not doing battle with a straw man? Or is she – and this is what I'm afraid of – debunking those of us who do wonder from time to time what the Great Mystery ahead of us might be like? I make no apology for being such a wonderer. Not to wonder in such a way strikes me as unnatural.

Third, she is correct in saying that our first concern should be following the Golden Rule and practicing compassion. Who would disagree with that? But it is quite another thing to claim that religion should restrict itself to ethics and never get around to metaphysics. There is plenty of room and time for both, and most serious Christians, Muslims, Hindus, Buddhists, and Sikhs – who comprise the membership of the world's five largest religions – make time for both.

Fourth, she is correct in saying that the world religions refer to and recommend practices that can lead to union with the Divine and to mystical ecstasy. But such experiences, with only rare exceptions, are available only to those who make religion the focus of their lives. Don't speak of such ecstasy to the Bolivian peasant hoeing his cassava or the American stockbroker managing to get herself and her kid to church every other Sunday. As the Buddha rightly said, most of life is unsatisfactory. Most of us rejoice in our faith that there is life after death because we find ourselves, let's be frank, somewhat unfulfilled in this life. People who claim to be indifferent to eternal life might be kidding themselves. Busy with the living of life, they might not have taken the time to consider what it means to be extinct – or rather, for *them* to be extinct.

Fifth, she is wrong to imply that an informed intellectual would have to be, like her, an agnostic on the subject of life after death. She is overlooking a massive amount of evidence that points to a personal afterlife. The literature written by doctors and psychologists on the near-death experience, the books written by hospice personnel about the extraordinary visions that dying people who are not doped up with painkillers commonly report, and the reports of spirits speaking through mediums, such as we've examined here, point to a mysterious dimension that exists alongside ours. One needs no faith to appreciate and weigh this evidence, only an open mind uncontaminated by materialist presuppositions. Has Armstrong done her homework in this area?

Armstrong aside for a moment, how much importance should

we assign to the afterlife? As a younger man I once broke up a party with the question, 'What do you guys think happens after death?' As an older man I find the subject, even in a religious studies department, better avoided. The subject seems to be surrounded by an aura of disrepute. We can talk about God, we can talk about ethics all day long, but the one subject that should most concern us – because everything else ultimately rests on it – is off limits among the smarter set where I work. I get the sense that faith in life after death is OK, but just don't *talk* about it, don't *admit* it. It's unsavory! Why is this?

I am quite sure I know. Among people who like to think of themselves as smart and well informed, such as you find among professors at a secular university, the materialist assumptions of the physical sciences color almost everything else. And since an afterlife is immaterial, at least in the way science understands matter, my colleagues are reluctant to admit they believe in it even if they do. Among them are two Catholics in the biology department, and one is a long-time friend. He deflects every attempt by prying students to learn if he is a man of faith, and in fact he implies that he is not. This is a man who loves his religion; but he is afraid to admit it. He doesn't want to look like a fool. He doesn't want to appear disreputable.

C. S. Lewis once said, 'It is since Christians have largely ceased to think of the other world that they have become so ineffective in this.' This is a claim that modern Christians, and the rest of us, need to ponder. Alongside Christianity's profound commitment to enjoying and bettering the world we live in now, is an unabashedly bold affirmation of a better world to follow. Skeptics think the two can't coexist, or at least they work at cross purposes. The world's major religions have wisely taught otherwise: A bold commitment to this world stands on the shoulders of a faith in the next. The spirits we have looked at here completely endorse this view. It is my hope that you will too.

Key References

Barker, Elsa (1995). *Letters from the Afterlife*. Hillsboro, Oregon: Beyond Words.

Betty, Stafford (2006). Life After Death Is Not a Red Herring. *America*, 195, 25-26.

Borgia, Anthony (no date). *Life in the World Unseen*. San Francisco: H. G. White.

Chism, Stephen (2005). *The Afterlife of Leslie Stringfellow*. Fayetteville, Arkansas: Fullcourte Press.

Cummins, Geraldine (1955). *The Road to Immortality*. London: Aquarian Press.

Greaves, Helen (1977). *Testimony of Light*. Saffron Walden, England: C. W. Daniel.

Moses, W. Stainton (1976). *Spirit Teachings*. New York: Arno Press.

Taylor, R. Mattson (1980). *Witness from Beyond*. South Portland, Maine: Foreword Press.

Taylor, R. Mattson (1999). *Evidence from Beyond*. Brooklyn, NY: Brett Books.

www.geocities.com/spirit_teachings/

Select Bibliography

Beloff, J. (1990). *The Relentless Question: Reflections on the Paranormal.* London: McFarland & Company.

Crookall, R. (1961). *The Supreme Adventure.* Cambridge, England: James Clarke.

Cummins, G. (1965). *Swan on a Black Sea.* London: Routledge and Kegan Paul.

Doyle, A. C. (1975). *The History of Spiritualism,* Vol. I. New York: Arno Press.

Fodor, N. (1966). *Encyclopaedia of Psychic Science.* New Hyde Park, NY: University Books.

Fontana, D. (2005). *Is There an Afterlife?* Ropley, Hants, UK: O Books.

Fontana, D. (2009). *Life Beyond Death.* London: Watkins

Garrett, E. (1975). *My Life As a Search for the Meaning of Mediumship.* New York: Arno Press.

Gauld, A. (1968). *The Founders of Psychical Research.* London: Routledge & Kegan Paul.

Hare, R. (1855). *Experimental Investigation of the Spirit Manifestations: Demonstrating the Existence of Spirits and Their Communion with Mortals.* New York: Partridge & Brittan.

Heath, R. H. and Klimo, J. (2006). *Suicide: What Really Happens in the Afterlife.* Berkeley: North Atlantic Books.

Heath, R. H. and Klimo, J. (2010). *Handbook to the Afterlife.* Berkeley: North Atlantic Books.

Heywood, R. (1974). *Beyond the Reach of Sense.* New York: E. P. Dutton.

Hick, J. (1980). *Death and Eternal Life.* San Francisco: Harper & Row.

Jacobson, N. (1971). *Life Without Death?* New York: Dell Publishing.

Johnson, R. (1971). *The Imprisoned Splendour.* Wheaton, Illinois:

Theosophical Publishing.

Kardec, A. (2003). *The Spirits' Book.* Philadelphia: Allan Kardec Educational Society.

Klimo, J. (1998). *Channeling: Investigations on Receiving Information from Paranormal Sources.* Berkeley: North Atlantic Books.

LaGrand, Louis (1997). *After Death Communication.* St. Paul, MN: Llewellyn.

Lewis, H. D. (1973). *The Self and Immortality.* New York: Seabury Press.

Lodge, O. (1915). *Raymond or Life and Death.* New York: George H. Doran.

Lodge, O. (1908). *Science and Immortality.* New York: Moffat, Yard and Company.

Matheson, R. (2004). *What Dreams May Come: A Novel.* New York: Tor Books.

Myers, F. W. H. (1961). *Human Personality and Its Survival of Bodily Death.* New Hyde Park, NY: University Books.

Roberts, J. (1978). *The Afterdeath Journal of an American Philosopher.* Englewood Cliffs, NJ: Prentice-Hall.

Schwartz, G. (2002). *The Afterlife Experiments.* New York: Pocket Books.

Smith, H. (1976). *Forgotten Truth: The Primordial Tradition.* San Francisco: Harper & Row.

Swedenborg, E. (1976). *Heaven and Hell.* New York: Pillar Books.

Tymn, M. (2008). *The Articulate Dead.* Lakeville, Minnesota: Galde Press.

Tymn, M. ed. (2002–10). *The Searchlight* (quarterly). Bloomfield, Connecticut: Academy of Spirituality and Paranormal Studies.

Tymn, M. (2007–10). http://metgat.gaia.com/blog.

Tymn, M. (2010–). http://whitecrowbooks.com/michaeltymn.

Whitton, J. and Fisher, F. (1986). *Life Between Life.* New York: Warner Books.

Wickland, C. (1974). *30 Years Among the Dead.* Hollywood, CA: Newcastle Publishing.

Wilson, C. (2000). *After Life: Survival of the Soul.* St. Paul, Minnesota: Llewellyn Publications.

Index

A
addiction 31,42,92,93
adoration 19
Afterlife of Leslie Stringfellow, The 26
anger 41,42,78,94
Animal-man 53,54
animals 18,27,97
arbitration in the afterlife 109
Archbishop of Canterbury 61
Armstrong, Karen 116-118
arts 28,45,54,67
astral body 54,56,82,83,91,103,108
astral clothing 67,90,108
astral world 2,9,46,81,89,91,103,105,108
atheists 8
Atlantis 35
aura 84
Avernus 20

B
Banks, Frances 75-87,87,109
Barker, Elsa 36,37,41,47,119
beach 65
Beautiful Being 36,40,47,108
beauty 2,16,37,40,45,53,55,68,72,73,8 1-86,90,102
Benson, Monsignor Robert

Hugh 61- 74,102,105,106,108,110,111
bestiality 71
Bettie, cousin 30
Bible 8,13
birds 18,27,97
blueprints 77,104,105
boats 65
Borgia, Anthony 61,62,74,110
Buddha 117
Buddhists 57,96,107,117
buildings 28,33,64,73,95

C
Calvary 13
Calvin, John 8
Catholics 96,114,115,118
challenges of earth 46
children 33,34,38,46,108
China 26
Chinese 32
Christ 13,24,39,83,95,107,108
Christianity 13,24,62,95,118
Christians 3, 8,22,24,63,96,108,110,113,116- 108
Christmas 29,30,63,108
churches 74,91
cities 20,24,27,28,35,64,65,67,102
clothing in the afterlife 108

counseling 67

creature comforts 45

comedies 66

Creator 104,112

creeds 62,69,83,107,108

cruelty 52-53

Cummins, Geraldine
4,48,49,119,120

D

dancing 81,82

danger, absence of 105

Dante 3,70,114

Davis, Jefferson 28

Day of Judgment, allegory 22

death
15,37,42,43,52,74,76,87,93,103,
104,108,110-114,118

death course 6

denial of death 103

density 76

desert country 70

despair 56,112

divine plan 104,112,114,115

dogma 69,83,107,108

dogmatism 13,93

Doyle, Arthur Conan 26

dream 51,81

drunkenness 20,42

E

Earth at center 63

earth-bound spirits 21,90,93

Easter 13,44,63,108

eating 105

Edward, John 2

Epiphany 62

eternity 45,48,58,74,115,116

Evidence from Beyond 88,99

evidential 5,26,37,89

evolution, spiritual
45,59,100,101,114

Exeter Cathedral 76

F

festivals of music 87

Fifth Plane (Myers) 58

Flavell, Margaret 88-90

flowers
16,18,27,29,30,32,55,63,68,70,7
3,76,81,85,90

food 18,91

forgiveness 8,75,93,109

Fourth Plane (Myers) 54-58

Franklin, Benjamin 28

free will 104,106

friendliness 73

friendships in the afterlife 107

fundamentalists 6

G

Galveston 34

gardens 65,67,76,81,84,87,102

God
6,8,11,13,14,19,22,27,31,32,33,
45,58,59,62,70,71,76,81,83,86,9
5,96,98,102,105,106,108,
109,113,114,115,118

Golden Rule 116
Greaves, Helen 4,75,76,79
grief 2
Group Soul 57,58,84,97

H
Hades 50,51
Halls of Learning 85
Hall of Literature 65
Hammarskjold, Dag 113
happiness, the way to 59,60
Hartley Productions 89
Hatch, Judge David 36-47,108,109,116
heaven(s) 3,13-15,33,40,41,43,45,56,58,72,76,81,86,102,108,113,114
hatred 21,41,42,56,77,109
hell(s) 3,13,15,20,22,30,31,41,42,76-80,90,106,109,113,114
Hindus 32,96,117
history 65
hobbies 46
homebuilding 45
homeownership 72
homesickness 109
homosexuality 100
houses 64,67
Huxley, Aldous 1

I
illness, absence of 105
Imperator 11-24,106,109,114

India 26,32
interpenetration of worlds 17,26,41,63,102

J
Jeannie 80-82
Jeans, Sir James 102
Jesus 13,24,45,62,63,75,83,95,108,109
Jewish mother 77,109
Jews 95,96,115
joy(s) 7,20,21,29,40,41,46,53,56,68,79,81,85,91,93,96,102,105,108,109,113,114,118
judgment 77,105
justice 2,104,114
Julian of Norwich 75

K
karma 57,71,72,81,114
knitting 46,109

L
lake 90,95
landscape 9,18,52,102,103,106
laughter 66,71,108
Letters from the Afterlife (Barker) 36
levitation 11
Lewis, C. S. 79,116,118
libraries 5,65,67,90,102
Life in the World Unseen 61

Light 80, 82-87
Lionel 46
Lincoln, Abraham 115
loneliness 30
love
  14,19,32,33,34,39,40,52,53,75,79,83,94-97,104,105,107
Luther, Martin 96,97

M
Mary Martin 31
masks 82,84,107
Masters 45
materialism 3, 6,118
Matheson, Richard 7
Mattson, AD 88-101,104,109,111
matter, subtle 43,46
meditation groups 85
mediums 1-13,26,30,36,48-50,61,62,79,88,103,104,110-112,117,120
mediumship, the process 50
memorial service, witness of 76
Mentor 16
Messiahs 39
Michelangelo 28
mind in the astral 106
ministers of the Church 69
missionary in Africa 79
missionary spirits
  20,22,70,79,106
More Spirit Teachings 12,24
Moses, Stainton
  4,11,12,16,17,18,22,23,49
Mother Teresa 113
Mountain of Fine Arts 28
Mozart 28
Muhammad 83
music 16,25,28,29,32-34,57,67,68,87,91,95,98,105
Muslims 6,107,117
Myers, Frederic 49-60,84,90,106,109,114,115

N
Nazi 77,109
near-death experience (NDE) 9
Necromancers, The 61
nihilism 3

O
occupations 19,67-69,85,90
omniscience 103
orphans 33,34,108

P
pageants 66
painter(s) 45,77-79
parties 29
pattern world 41
Pentecost 62
pets 90,97
Pius X, Pope Saint 61
planchette 25
Plane of Illusion 51-54
planetary gods 39
planets, inhabited 47,54,98,104

play 66,91
polio 80
prayers for the dead 85,108
precious stones 73
progress in the Afterlife, how
     to 107
purgatory 3,15,41,76,86,114
purpose of existence
     59,60,101,104

R
reading 35,89,106
Realm of the Unprogressed
     30,31
Rector 19
religion
     1,12,14,24,31,32,62,74,83,94,1
     08,116-118
Revelations of Divine Love 75
reincarnation
     3,22,23,43,44,57,58,74,82,83,9
     9,100,109-111
Resurrection 13,103
rituals of music105
roads 64,102
Road to Immortality, The 49

S
salvation 32,83,95
Satan 21
scientists 2,68
seven planes (Myers) 49,50
seven spheres (Imperator) 15
Seventh Plane (Myers) 59

sex 40,53,100,106
Shadowlands 7,77,84,90,106
Sherlock Holmes 26
Sikhs 117
sin(s) 13,15,20,22,41,93,94
Sixth Plane (Myers) 58
sleep 92,105
Society for Psychical Research
     9,49
soil 63,64
Soul-man 53-55
soul-building 104
space travel 97,98
spheres of contemplation 16
spheres of debased spirits 19
spheres of probation 17
spirit adversaries 20,21
spirit guides 69,70
Spirit-man 53
Spirit Teachings 12,24
spirits, demented 71
Spiritualism 120
Spiritualists 24,27,110
sport 66,67
Stevenson, Ian 111
Stringfellow, Alice 25,26,30,31
Stringfellow, Leslie 25-
     35,41,51,63,74,108
suffering 14,42,52,56,117
suicide 109
Summerland 27-30,32,33,51

T
Taylor, Ruth Mattson 88,99

teaching 19,67
telepathy 33,68,85,92,103,105
teleportation 103
Testimony of Light 6,75,85
theatre 106
Third Plane (Myers) 52-54
time 14,19,63,74,107,109
Tom Jones 52
traffic 64,102
travel 28,29,32,85,97-99,104
trees 16,27,28,32-34,65,70,85,95
two wives, dilemma 43

U
universities 102

unpardonable sin 22

V
vibration(s) 55,86,90,102-104
violence 66
visions 7

W
war 92
water 16,64,65,68,73,90
What Dreams May Come 7
Wilberforce, Bishop 18
Williams, Robin 7
Witness from Beyond 88,89,99

BOOKS

O is a symbol of the world, of oneness and unity. In different cultures it also means the "eye," symbolizing knowledge and insight. We aim to publish books that are accessible, constructive and that challenge accepted opinion, both that of academia and the "moral majority."

Our books are available in all good English language bookstores worldwide. If you don't see the book on the shelves ask the bookstore to order it for you, quoting the ISBN number and title. Alternatively you can order online (all major online retail sites carry our titles) or contact the distributor in the relevant country, listed on the copyright page.

See our website **www.o-books.net** for a full list of over 500 titles, growing by 100 a year.

And tune in to myspiritradio.com for our book review radio show, hosted by June-Elleni Laine, where you can listen to the authors discussing their books.

MySpiritRadio